33 WAYS GOD *is* PREPARING *the* WORLD *for the* SECOND COMING

ALSO BY THIS AUTHOR

The Complete Idiot's Guide to Understanding Mormonism

33 WAYS GOD *is* PREPARING *the* WORLD *for the* SECOND COMING

DREW WILLIAMS

CFI

An imprint of Cedar Fort, Inc.
Springville, Utah

ISBN 13: 978-1-4621-2203-5

Published by CFI, an imprint of Cedar Fort, Inc.
2373 W. 700 S., Springville, UT 84663
Distributed by Cedar Fort, Inc., www.cedarfort.com

LIBRARY OF CONGRESS CONTROL NUMBER: 2018941189

Cover design by Shawnda T. Craig
Cover design © 2018 Cedar Fort, Inc.

Printed in the United States of America

10 9 8 7 6 5 4 3 2 1

Printed on acid-free paper

DEDICATION

For Carter Thomas, in whose eyes I see eternal hope.

Contents

ACKNOWLEDGMENTS

I acknowledge all of those amazing teachers of the Holy Bible with whom I have had the privilege of studying. From the first time I sat on my grandmother's lap as a child as she read passages from the New Testament, I was captured by the words and verses. Many times I have had the opportunity to share healthy discussions with Christian scholars over the teachings of Isaiah, Jesus, and John the Revelator. With every discussion, every Sunday School and religion class over the years, I have always found the Holy Bible to be my own personal cornerstone to my faith as a Christian and as a Latter-day Saint convert.

Now, with gratitude and a slight blend of anxiety and an extra dose of humility, I express my sincere gratitude to my dear wife, Sallie, for her unwavering support "in sickness and in health." Your valiance and dedication to service reflects in everything you do, and I am grateful for your companionship. You still make me smile whenever I see you walk into a room!

Also, to sweet Shirley (aka "Sylvia"), who, at eighty-six years old, has always marched to a different drummer, while all the while remaining steadfast in her faith that a loving Redeemer will be there for all of us in the end.

To those powerful spiritual influences of my life: the late, great Bill Pope, who never apologized for his faith in God; to Jack Christianson, who looks the other way when I want to nudge my golf ball just a little; and to my precious Carolina Grace, who is a gem among my most sacred treasures.

FOREWORD

For many years, Drew Williams and I have worked together at a university, played golf together, critiqued various writing projects together, and most important, discussed religious matters together. Therefore, when he asked me to write a foreword for his newest work, *33 Ways God Is Preparing the World for the Second Coming*, I was honored.

As I read through much of the manuscript, I realized that this book is unlike anything I have read concerning the last dispensation. Drew added his unique writing style that allowed me, the reader, to appreciate him as the author and his personality, along with the well-researched material presented on each page. As he interjected his comments intermittently, it gave a tone to the book that gently prodded me to continue reading. It made the book not only eye opening but also enjoyable to read. I found myself hearing him talk as I read the powerful words about preparing for the time period that men and women have looked forward to for centuries.

The other unique factor, for me, was his drawing upon the Old and New Testaments and very little else for his reference material. His use of the scriptures gave the book an authoritative feel that is so needed in these times of indecision and wandering from the path of truth and righteousness.

Our day has been the topic of numerous ancient prophets and teachers, including the Savior Jesus Christ himself. This book is valuable for all members of The Church of Jesus Christi of Latter-day Saints, as well as members of all faiths throughout the world.

I am a better person for having read this volume. My hope is that each reader will be benefited and blessed as I have been. As you prayerfully read through each chapter, may you be motivated and inspired to better prepare with full purpose of heart for this last dispensation!

—Jack R. Christianson, PhD
Motivational author and speaker

INTRODUCTION

*God writes the gospel
not in the Bible alone.[1]*

—Martin Luther

While many Christian groups throughout the world believe the Holy Bible to be the word of God as it has been translated, historians and scholars continue to identify the many inconsistencies and misinterpretations of this holy writ that have transpired over thousands of years, and the fundamental belief is that this ancient body of work is only part of God's continued dialog with the human race. Although some religious scholars would defend a more official position that the Bible is an integral component of the principal precepts of a larger core body of Judeo-Christian philosophy, the words and passages of the Bible are often seen as complicated, convoluted, and ambiguous. But not for me!

For Christians throughout the world, the Holy Bible is the decisive source for all things relating to the word of God, while for others, additional or alternative words mean just as much (if not more). Often, however, and certainly in the LDS community, all references to the Bible fall in the shadows of the Book of Mormon and the other components of the standard works not written in the Mesopotamian delta.

While library and bookstore shelves are well stocked with studies and treatises on the various virtues of "scripture," this book focuses exclusively on historical and biblical references as they pertain to supporting the thirty-three essays that are presented as the main body of this work. This book does not attempt to reveal any earth-shaking or life-altering passages of yet-to-be-discovered meaning in the words of doctrine, nor does this body of work attempt to justify the historicity of an ancient people.

This book is presented as a matter of reference and observations made regarding thirty-three various topics pertaining to Christian eschatology and the anticipation of a time in which the promised Messiah will return, rule, and restore his kingdom on the earth. Its research centers around the Old and New Testaments, as well as historical accounts of various entities from antiquity, and it is hoped to be a reminder of how important and relevant the ancient passages found in the Holy Bible remain in a world of continued uncertainty and increasing ambiguity.

Remember, this is from the perspective of one person (me) and by no means is a definitive study on anything. But, wow! It was sure fun to write!

—Drew Williams

NOTE

1. Attributed to Martin Luther. See https://www.brainyquote.com/quotes/martin
_luther_140721. Accessed May 17, 2018.

PART I

A MILLENNIUM OF SOCIAL EVOLUTION THROUGH THE WRITTEN WORD

Non acer Asylum autem in claustro.

No asylum but in the cloister. (Domesday Book[1])

The distribution of early Christian thought, philosophy, and culture was the fastest way to impart knowledge and enlightenment throughout the civilizations of Europe. There was, perhaps, no greater influence on medieval society than the creation (and controversy) of a device that society hoped would liberate them from the tight control of religious dictates and political bias. In 1438, a German blacksmith refined an ancient Asian printing technique by which moveable type could be reset into a device to mass-produce written materials.

Thanks to Johannes Gutenberg, and having the good fortune of him bringing his printing modifications to a culturally expanding central Europe, the dawn of enlightenment brought literacy to a new generation. Gutenberg's printing[2] of the illuminated version of the Latin Vulgate Bible in 1455 opened a floodgate for commoners to gain access to religious dogma, literature, and legal documents that were otherwise not available to anyone but the church or the local regents.

Before Gutenberg, however, and for those of European—and more specifically—English/Norman descent, no public document has held more historical value to documenting the day-to-day life of our distant past than that of the volume known as the "Domesday Book"[3] of William the Conqueror. Compiled in 1086 and commissioned by England's first united regent, the land survey included what was to be considered the definitive census of all humans, livestock, land, and materials throughout Britain. It has been used throughout the centuries in land disputes and treaty reviews, with the last such quarrel being settled as recent as the early twentieth century.

The Domesday Book (or Doomsday) was one of several key documents that changed the face of early medieval civilization in Christian Europe. With the unifying of the barons of England against King John under the Magna Carta of 1215, the idea of any one person being above the law became a thing of the past (in theory), although that line blurred the closer you got to the crown or the Vatican.

————

Notes

1. See The National Archives, https://nationalarchives.gov.uk/documents/education/domesday .pdf to download a free copy of the Domesday Book. (Courtesy of The National Archives.) Accessed April 24, 2018.
2. Owlcation, Amanda Littlejohn, "Johannes Gutenberg and the Printing Press: Social & Cultural Impact," https://owlcation.com/humanities/Johannes-Gutenberg-and-the -Printing-Press-Revolution. Accessed April 24, 2018.
3. Encyclopedia Britannica, "Domesday Book," https://www.britannica.com/topic/Domesday -Book. Accessed April 24, 2018.

CHAPTER 1

GOD'S SPIRIT POURED OUT ON ALL FLESH

Old men shall dream dreams.

—Joel 2:28

And so, we begin.

When starting out a book that attempts to look at the fate of mankind by mapping our inevitable destiny with a handful of historical and biblical references, it's probably a good idea to anchor such concepts and suppositions on the notion that "God told me to do it."

Well, okay, not exactly, but here's the idea: whenever any major life-changing event in history has come to pass (I'm talking about the really big ones), more often than not there's a connection to some foreshadowing by divine prophecy.[1]

The idea, for example, that our calendar[2] is tied to the birth of Jesus Christ has transcended from the religious fancy of the Dark Ages to a general standard across most of modern civilization. This idea is relatively young in comparison to the epoch of time. (Only since the 1700s has the current calendar been considered the "standard" for measuring time.) Although more with Christian followers than those who back scientific calculations, the notion of using the birth of Jesus has become something of an accepted assumption by more than two billion people:[3] "There is a God, he lived two thousand years ago, and our world has never been the same because of it," just as the biblical prophets of old foresaw!

As foretold by those Jewish sages of the Old Testament, and after Israel wandered for thousands of years and was persecuted by its neighbors, he who would ransom himself for the fate of mankind came into the world, and upon his birth, framed the very nature of time immemorial.

For I am God, and there is none else; I am God, and there is none like me, declaring the end from the beginning. (Isaiah 46:9–10)

More than three hundred references in the Old Testament foreshadow the coming of the Messiah. Just as Isaiah foretold more than seven hundred years earlier,[4] young *Yeshua ben Yosef* (the proper Jewish name[5] of the infant child called "Jesus") was born in less than favorable conditions, in a small outpost community of the ancient Roman Empire, in a land where people were coerced to worship a host of characters.

And mankind has never been the same.

Was this event the beginning of what Isaiah writes and describes as "a marvelous work?"

> I will proceed to do a marvelous work among this people, even a marvelous work and a wonder: for the wisdom of their wise men shall perish, and the understanding of their prudent men shall be hid. (Isaiah 29:14)

By the time he was fourteen, the teenage Jesus was walking and studying—and teaching—among the scholars of his time.[6] This otherwise obscure son of a carpenter soon rose to become a controversial figure that was yoked with both praise and condemnation—neither of which were asked for or deserved.

What, then, gave the first inkling that these so-called "dispensations" had to come to pass, and why claim we are now in the final throes of mortality?

We begin by turning to another Old Testament prophet, Joel, for indications that these days of monumental storms of earth, wind, fire, and rain may actually be marking the closing chapters on the saga of man.

> And it shall come to pass afterward, that I will pour out my spirit upon all flesh; and your sons and your daughters shall prophesy, your old men shall dream dreams, your young men shall see visions. . . . I will shew wonders in the heavens and in the earth, blood, and fire, and pillars of smoke. The sun shall be turned into darkness, and the moon into blood, before the great and terrible day of the Lord come. (Joel 2:28, 30–31)

As our world now finds itself amidst the teenage years of the twenty-first century, the news of the day reveals more often than not new scientific and technological advances that have been otherwise only thought of as science fiction in medicine, communications, transportation, space exploration, and conflict. But in the adolescence of the 2000s, amidst torrential destruction, fire storms, and an abundance of "rumors of war," the wisest among us have always turned to signs in history to foresee the signs of the times. Automobiles now race to beyond three hundred miles per hour, aircraft fly beyond five times the speed of sound, scientists have learned to harness the power of a single atom, and man has reached other planets.

In this age of everything, based on an equation developed by the twentieth century architect Buckminster Fuller, the human race is said to double in knowledge every twelve months,[7] as was prophesied by Daniel:

O Daniel, shut up the words, and seal the book, even to the time of the end: many shall run to and fro, and knowledge shall be increased. (Daniel 12:4)

Now, in a time of "increased knowledge," when nations continue to rise against nations, trying to map the time frame for the great and dreadful day of the Lord is something of a paradox. What will be the final stroke of the pen on mortality? What will trigger those final closing moments when, as was written by the Apostle James almost two millennia ago, the coming of the Lord is at hand?[8]

This book was born out of a desire to develop a better understanding of the nature of man and God from a purely biblical and historical context. Each of the thirty-three chapters offers a brief individual sketch on some aspect of the idea that history as we know it has been part of a progressive and divine plan; that mankind is running out of time to figure out why we're here and what we need to do to get to the next phase of eternity.

The term *eschatology*[9] is used to describe the death, judgment, and final outcome of the human soul. Christian eschatology focuses largely on the final outcome and afterlife of mortality, as well as heaven and hell, the return of Jesus (the Second Coming), the Resurrection of those who have died, the end of the world, the Final Judgment, and the belief that a new heaven and earth will replace the current conditions we experience in mortality. The Bible is replete with numerous eschatological passages that are in both the Old and New Testaments, as well as in apocryphal writings from periods throughout ancient history.

While by no means a definitive discourse on the subject, this book attempts, through historical, biblical, and eschatological references, to shed some light on important markers along the way, from the days of Isaiah and Joel through the Norman Conquest and all the way up to present day.

Following his Resurrection and after a short return visit to the Holy Land, Jesus gathered his Apostles one final time and told them that he would be leaving for a while. He promised he would return at an appropriate time in the not-so-distant future. Now, almost two thousand years since Jesus's departure, the Christian world still looks to the day of his return.

Some Christian faiths teach that the Second Coming of Christ opens the final chapter of the mortal probation of mankind. Jesus's return has been the subject of extensive debate almost since the moment he was carried into heaven after the day of Pentecost. Although many cultures today and throughout history declared their insider knowledge as to when the Lord will return, the Bible notes that even Christ himself does not know when God will send him back to close this final chapter.

So perhaps the question isn't "When will he come back?" Rather, "Will we be ready?"

Notes

1. Ligonier Ministries, "Divine Prophecy," https://www.ligonier.org/learn/devotionals/divine -prophecy/. Accessed April 23, 2018.
2. History Channel, Jennie Cohen, "6 Things You May Not Know About the Gregorian Calendar," http://www.history.com/news/6-things-you-may-not-know-about-the-gregorian -calendar, September 13, 2012. Accessed April 23, 2018.
3. *Washington Times*, Jennifer Harper, "84 Percent of the world population has faith; a third are Christian," https://www.washingtontimes.com/blog/watercooler/2012/dec/23/84 -percent-world-population-has-faith-third-are-ch/, December 23, 2012. Accessed April 23, 2018.
4. See Isaiah 53, King James Version of the Bible.
5. Hope of Israel Ministries, John D. Keyser, "What's the Messiah's REAL name?" http:// www.hope-of-israel.org/messiahsname.html. Accessed April 23, 2018.
6. See Luke 2:41–52, King James Version of the Bible.
7. Industry Tap, David Russell Schilling, "Knowledge Doubling Every 12 Months, Soon to be Every 12 Hours," http://www.industrytap.com/knowledge-doubling-every-12-months-soon -to-be-every-12-hours/3950, April 19, 2013. Accessed April 23, 2018.
8. See James 5:8, King James Version of the Bible.
9. Merriam-Webster Dictionary definition of "eschatology," https://www.merriam-webster .com/dictionary/eschatology. Accessed April 23, 2018.

Chapter 2

Discovery and Use of Printing

A spring of truth shall flow from it.[1]

—Johannes Gutenberg

When was the first time you read a good book?

Some people might think that the first time a book was actually printed and distributed was when Johannes Gutenberg constructed his printing press in the mid-1400s in Germany.

It must be acknowledged that Johannes Gutenberg's new technology helped introduce the word of God (as well as everything else that was printed at the time) to the West, but the process of moveable type had long been established throughout Asia.[2] In China, by the second century, craftsmen were imbedding ink onto paper using blocks. By the mid-800s, their technology was advanced enough to produce complete publications.

While historians and scholars continue to debate the intent, origins, and motives behind Gutenberg's work (he was never paid for the 180 copies of his Bible), most agree that the work surrounding what is now one of the most valuable and rare historical documents in the world[3] laid the groundwork for what would become the age of enlightenment.

By the end of the Middle Ages, which is usually marked by the fall of Constantinople[4] in 1453, Christianity was so much a part of the fabric of Western culture that there was little distinction between community and religion. Everything was influenced and aligned with the church—be it music, art, or even science.

But it is literature and the distribution of the written word that scholars suggest had the fastest influence on advancing Western thought following the Dark Ages. The leading publication, of course, was the Bible. Monks were producing illuminated copies of various passages throughout the fourteenth and fifteenth centuries to help spread the word of God to places where it had not yet been introduced.

Gutenberg's work with moveable type led to the new concept of mass communication, a concept that forever altered the way in which societies and civilizations would develop and how people learned, discussed, and believed. Gutenberg had this to say about it:

> It is a press, certainly, but a press from which shall flow in inexhaustible streams, the most abundant and most marvelous liquor that has ever flowed to relieve the thirst of men! Through it, God will spread His Word. A spring of truth shall flow from it: like a new star it shall scatter the darkness of ignorance and cause a light heretofore unknown to shine amongst men.[5] (Johannes Gutenberg)

The written word reorganizes how concepts regarding life, liberty, property, and even God are perceived, believed, and acted upon. As new concepts were distributed, those in-the-know began to expand. Where only wealthy religious leaders and royal families had been in control of ideas, a rising tide of reformation began to take hold of Central Europe, largely in part because of mass communication. Throughout the fifteenth and sixteenth centuries, as self-awareness began to reshape the way people looked at their respective leaders in the church and in their local governments, the sense of nationalism began to grow as the elitists who had been in control were now on even plains of understanding with commoners.

In Paul's first letter to the Corinthian Christians, he referenced the way that God grants special gifts to his children. God gives his gifts in a way that keeps both diversity and cooperation alive, while also advancing his word and his work. In 1 Corinthians we read,

> Now there are diversities of gifts, but the same Spirit. And there are differences of administrations, but the same Lord. And there are diversities of operations, but it is the same God which worketh all in all. But the manifestation of the Spirit is given to every man to profit withal. For to one is given by the Spirit the word of wisdom; to another the word of knowledge by the same Spirit; to another faith by the same Spirit; to another the gifts of healing by the same Spirit; to another the working of miracles; to another prophecy; to another discerning of spirits; to another divers kinds of tongues; to another the interpretation of tongues: But all these worketh that one and the selfsame Spirit, dividing to every man severally as he will. (1 Corinthians 12:4–11)

While in ancient times, the gospel and those who would follow it were validated by their respective deeds. Religious leaders would agree that such "diversities of operations" and spiritual manifestations to advance wisdom and knowledge were not reserved for the period of the ancient prophets. Although Gutenberg never affixed his name to any book he published, his tribute by Pope Pius II in 1455 reflects on the man's legacy as being someone who focused on quality in his work:

> All that has been written to me about that marvelous man seen at Frankfurt is true. I have not seen complete Bibles but only a number of quires of various books of the Bible. The script was very neat and legible, not at all difficult to follow—your grace would be able to read it without effort, and indeed without glasses.[6] (Pius II, 1455)

The mechanics of the press were only the instrument, albeit one of great impact on kick-starting the Reformation, Renaissance, and enlightenment era. With the open expression of thought and interpretation in the written word, societies were primed for a cultural revolution, and that's just what happened.

Where friars and monks would have otherwise worked for days sequestered in their scriptoria[7] to hand-publish one work, and then only in portions, the printing press with its moveable type was able to produce hundreds of manuscripts in their entirety in a matter of hours. This allowed people more flexibility and access to knowledge across a wide range of topics. It also provided religious leaders the ability to spread their versions of the gospel and subsequently expand their locus of influence (and often their sway of personal and political bias) over larger congregations.

The Catholic Church almost immediately recognized the power of the written word and how it would influence and alter the mind, conscience, and motivations of society. Within forty years of Gutenberg's advancements in printing, Rome began requiring all books—religious as well as secular—to be screened and approved prior to being published. Although church censorship of publications had been present for hundreds of years, once the ability to publish thousands of copies of a manuscript was achieved, the church no longer had control over what was published. Keeping central messages about faith, God, and fealty under the church's jurisdiction would be akin to herding birds in a windstorm.

Adding to Rome's anxiety, the most sacred of all books—the Bible—was now being translated from Latin into various *vulgar* tongues of local dialects across Europe, which in turn also meant interpreting different perspectives of gospel stories, passages, psalms, and histories based on syntax, word choice, and tribal interpretation of the stories.

Printing in local dialects meant more people would have access to read something other than Latin. The expanding reading public included women, who were, in general, never allowed to learn to read.

Because of the advancement of mass printing, the way in which individual words were spelled became consistent, which provided a common context for even further translation of more texts. Ultimately, Latin became an archaic language, retreating to the halls of churches and universities.

By the time Columbus had reached the New World, Gutenberg's innovations in printing had spread throughout Europe to Italy, London, and Paris. Along with the mass production of biblical passages (such as the Psalter,[8] which was a book of Old Testament Psalms), other religious works by the likes of Lacantius and Josephus and classical stories from history (such as the *Iliad* and *Odyssey*, historical treatises from Emperor Charlemagne, and the works of Chaucer and Dante) were reaching the masses.

By 1500, more than twenty-five hundred cities throughout Europe had acquired printing presses. With the propagation of mass printing came the stimulation of curiosity, which led to deeper understanding of how life worked (both in the church as well as throughout the various fiefdoms of Europe). Critical thinking, scholarship, and philosophy became consistent, while expanding to embrace more cultures and infuse more ideologies.

Enter Dr. Martin Luther.

In 1517, Luther, a Catholic priest and professor of moral theology in Saxon-Germany, wrote, printed, published, and distributed his "95 Theses,"[9] also referred to as the "Disputation on the Power of Efficacy and Indulgences," which included arguments regarding the compensation of Catholic priests (called "indulgences") for hearing and forgiving a range of transgressions by their respective parishioners. The December 1517 printing of Luther's theses went viral, and, as a result, the Protestant reformation was born.

————

NOTES

1. The Blazing Center, Mark Altrogge, "The Passion of Gutenberg," https://theblazingcenter.com/2013/07/give-me-more-of-gutenbergs-passion.html, July 29, 2013. Accessed April 26, 2018. See also the Crandall Historical Printing Museum's website, http://www.crandallprintingmuseum.org/gutenberg-to-grandin.html. Accessed April 23, 2018.

2. Elation Press, "Short History of Asia's Influence on Type and Printing," http://elationpress.com/resources/short-history-of-asias-influence-on-type-and-printing/. Accessed April 23, 2018.

3. Currently only twenty-one complete copies of the Gutenberg Bible are in existence, with an estimated value of approximately $30 million. Individual pages of the fourteen-pound book currently fetch between $50,000 and $150,000, depending on the page and its quality. See Bookriot, E. H. Kern, "10 Things You Should Know about the Gutenberg Bible," https://bookriot.com/2016/07/13/10-things-you-should-know-about-the-gutenberg-bible/, July 13, 2016. Accessed May 17, 2018.

4. Encyclopedia Britannica, Tony Bunting, "Fall of Constantinople," https://www.britannica.com/event/Fall-of-Constantinople-1453. Accessed April 24, 2018.

5. Altrogge, "The Passion of Gutenberg."

6. WikiVisually, "Gutenberg Bible," https://wikivisually.com/wiki/Gutenberg_Bible. Accessed April 23, 2018.

7. Encyclopedia Britannica, "Scriptorium," https://www.britannica.com/art/scriptorium. Accessed April 23, 2018.

8. Protestant Reformed Churches in America, "The Psalter as Used for Public Worship in the PRCA," http://www.prca.org/resources/worship-devotional/psalter. Accessed April 23, 2018.

9. See http://www.champs-of-truth.com/reform/LUT_95TH.PDF to download a free copy of Martin Luther's "The 95 Theses." (Courtesy of Champs of Truth website.) Other websites also offer it free. Search "95 Theses" in your browser to find them. Accessed April 23, 2018.

CHAPTER 3

PROTESTANT REFORMATION

In the hope of the promised Messiah!

While the Greek Orthodox faction of Catholicism controlled much of Greece and Eastern Europe, the strong grip of traditional Catholic influence over intellectual, religious, and political thought by Rome throughout Central and Western Europe was weakening by the mid-sixteenth century.

The post-medieval Roman Catholic Church in the sixteenth century was rife with controversy—thanks in part to commoners now having the opportunity to learn to read. They no longer chose to follow one singular (and often mandated) frame of thought about how things should transpire in life and in the fields—and in the church.

Throughout the prior fifteen hundred years, the church—especially with respect to the Pope, his cardinals, and their respective lieutenants—had swayed the government landscape throughout Europe. The subsequent conspiracies and partisan influences, combined with the dramatic rise in power, wealth, and control by Rome, ultimately led to the church's authority being compromised, which resulted in its loss of control over the spiritual component of life for many disaffected parishioners.

A rise in financial abuse (because of the peddling of spiritual liberties and absolutions called "indulgences") led to mass corruption as well, further expanding the schism between the faithful and leadership.

Throughout sixteenth century Europe, the spread of doubt over the teachings of the church began to take hold among the religious scholars and influencers. Some religious historians suggest the impetus behind the rise in controversy is tied to translations of the original texts—specifically those by fourth century Christian philosopher Augustine—as well as others from the early church.

Rather than focus on the influence of church leadership, Augustine stressed the pre-eminence of scriptural relevance as being the ultimate guidepost for spiritual authority. Another principal argument introduced by Augustine was the notion that the human race could not make it back to God's presence based on their good deeds. He believed that salvation was bestowed on each of us by the grace of God. This striking concept was a stark contrast to medieval Catholicism, which emphasized the idea that salvation was affixed to righteous works.

Martin Luther, who had become somewhat jaded from the practice of the church granting "indulgences" (for a fee), came to agree with Augustine's two-fold premises about salvation by grace and the scriptures (rather than religious leaders) representing the word of God. These core tenets would set the foundation on which Protestantism would be established.

Because he was dedicated to the notion that salvation came through grace (rather than by good works), Luther argued and opposed the further practice of granting indulgences, and, as part of his newfound faith in God's grace, authored the "Disputation on the Power and Efficacy of Indulgences" in 1517, which has been more commonly referred to as "The 95 Theses."[2] This list of rhetorical commentaries was posited as a means of initiating thought about how God, the church, its leaders, and the masses interacted, and how salvation was not a commodity that could be purchased. A sampling of Martin Luther's theses:

> Those who believe they can be certain of their salvation because they have letters of indulgence will in fact be eternally damned along with their teachers. . . . They who teach that contrition is not needed for those who intend to buy souls out of purgatory or to buy confessional privileges are preaching unchristian doctrine. . . . Any truly repentant Christian has a right to full remission of both the penalty and guilt, even without letters of indulgence. . . . Any true Christian, living or dead, participates in all the benefits of Christ and the Church. This is given to him by God, even without letters of indulgence.[3]

Thanks to the innovations brought forth by Gutenberg, Luther's "95 Theses" was mass-produced and distributed from Germany to Rome, which garnered the attention of a disgruntled papacy. A debate that was initiated by Imperial Order in 1518 saw Luther locking in a three-day argument with Cardinal Thomas Cajetan. The topic: indulgences and the defense of their use and support. Luther would have none of the Cardinal's claims, and he left the debate without resolution. Shortly after, the church under Pope Leo X issued a papal degree proclaiming Luther a heretic and his "95 Theses" "scandalous and offensive to pious ears."

By 1521, the Protestant Reformation had taken hold of central Europe and spread from the Baltic to the Atlantic, with the newfound Lutheranism becoming the state religion of Germany in 1524, as well as throughout the Scandinavian states.

With the rapid spread of the Reformation throughout Europe during the mid-sixteenth century, Lutheranism spawned other Protestant factions, including Anabaptists, who condemned the practice of infant baptism; Calvinists, who believed in the philosophy of predestination; and Socinians, who protested the original doctrine on the Holy Trinity. Despite the growing range in controversy surrounding the church, which ranged from ambivalence to outright rebellion, and the rise in support for the shift in religious thought led by the likes of Calvin and Luther, the Catholic Church did (and still does) remain a bulwark for spiritual strength for millions of followers.

Another development, which transitioned into a "state" problem for the church, was that at the beginning of the seventeenth century, under a Protestant king, the English crown and court began to aggressively stifle Rome's influence and broad control over public thought, which triggered further anxiety and conflict.

More than twelve hundred years after the first councils at Nicaea, and following centuries of religious bloodshed, conquests, and religious crusades, James VI of Scotland ascended to the throne of England[4] in 1603 and forever unified the two nations as King James I of Great Britain.

A pattern of enforced religious consistency and interpretation was about to resurface, which would consider how the faithful would interpret and follow the word of God—but with a twist. This boy king of Scotland and England was a student of religious writings in both Greek and Latin, as well as in the works of John Calvin. By the age of twelve, James was leading his government (with a few close advisers) and spurring on healthy debates regarding the puritanical nature of God at the Hampton Court Conference.[5]

Religious factions, however, were producing their own versions of what was to be called "scripture," along with individual charters for how to lead the faithful and pay the clergy. At his Hampton Court Conference,[6] James took charge and led discussions on matters concerning church government, prayer, and how to best translate the Bible.

James had wanted to unite the religious factions—Catholic and Protestant—in one unified base of doctrine under the auspices of the Church of England. Shadowing those efforts of the ancient Roman Emperor Constantine's councils some thirteen hundred years prior, the ruler of an empire again leveraged his political influence to establish a compromise between religious factions (with the added twist of everyone on both sides of the Catholic-Protestant debate agreeing to certain political conditions).

Political and religious unrest in Europe, however, began to go from a stir to a boil eighty years before James's move to unify the varied religious groups under one crown.

But by 1600, with the European Reformation in full swing, the Catholic Church was in a power struggle with the strident Protestant King from Scotland, and between 1604 and 1611, King James commissioned a group of scholars from throughout the British Empire to converge on Hampton Court and translate a new "authorized" version of the Holy Bible. Replacing what was commonly referred to as the Great Bible, which had stood as the common tome of holy writ for hundreds of years, King James's Authorized Version displaced the Latin Vulgate as the standard works for English-speaking students of the word of God—much to the chagrin of Rome.

The revised body of religious books followed Luther's lead and segregated what the Protestant king and his consorts considered "uninspired, spurious books written by various individuals" into an inter-testamental section entitled "Books called Apocrypha." These books, labeled "non-canonical" by Protestant leaders, were often included in the Protestant editions of the Bible of the times, but with the caveat that "These Books Are

Not Held Equal to the Scriptures but Are Useful and Good to Read."[7]

The Apocrypha[8] comprises fourteen books that were originally part of the Greek Old Testament (although not part of the Hebrew-written Bible) but were considered canon by Hellenist Jews who lived in foreign lands during the time of Christ. The nine "accepted" Apocryphal books include

- Ecclesiasticus[9]—Written 180 BC. This book includes proverbs and Hebrew life observations two centuries before the birth of Christ.

- Wisdom [of Solomon][10]—Many scholars hold up the book of Wisdom as one of the most significant of the Apocryphal collection. Written about 65 BC, Wisdom was designed as a counterpoint to what many within the Jewish sects believed to be the excessive worldliness found within the book of Ecclesiastes.

- 1 Maccabees[11]—Along with providing foundational literature for the Jewish festival of Hanukkah, this book by a Hebrew author living in Palestine was written two hundred years before Christ and documents the death of Simon and the Maccabean uprising.

- 2 Maccabees[12]—This story also describes the Maccabean rebellion.

- Tobit[13]—This popular book of fictional romance and philosophy was written around 300 BC. It is thought to be loosely based on two prominent Egyptian stories that also incorporate one of the Jewish archangels Raphael.

- Bel and the Dragon[14]—This apocryphal book traces its history to the time of Daniel and the legend of the Babylonian dragon idol-god. Written a century before the birth of Christ, the book of Tobit contains numerous references to future prophecies incorporating retribution.

- Judith[15]—Strong female figures are seldom referenced as prominently in the scriptures as Deborah, Ruth, and Naomi, but the book of Judith centers on a widow of great influence who overcomes her enemies after killing the leader of the Assyrian army.

- [Additions to] Esther[16]—Authors from the first century BC returned to the Old Testament text and added clarification to ambiguous passages in the original book of Esther, intending to add depth and further impress upon the faithful the magnitude of the struggle between God and the adversary in the last days.

- Baruch[17]—Named for and assumed written by Jeremiah's personal scribe, this book includes "The Epistle of Jeremiah."

While no longer considered canon by most non-Catholic Christians, there was a time when, before the Reformation, the sixteenth-century Bible (Geneva) considered the Apocryphal books to be read only as references.

The books . . . which were not received by a common consent to be read and expounded publicly in the Church, neither yet served to prove any point of Christian religion save in so much as they had the consent of the other scriptures called canonical to confirm the same, or rather whereon they were grounded: but as books proceeding from godly men they were received to be read for the advancement and furtherance of the knowledge of history and for the instruction of godly manners: which books declare that at all times God had an especial care of his Church, and left them not utterly destitute of teachers and means to confirm them in the hope of the promised Messiah, and also witness that those calamities that God sent to his Church were according to his providence, who had both so threatened by his prophets, and so brought it to pass, for the destruction of their enemies and for the trial of his children.[18] (Preface to the Apocrypha in the Geneva Bible)

Notes

1. From the Preface to the Apocrypha in the Geneva Bible. See http://www.apuritansmind .com/free-geneva-bible-downloads-and-other-bibles/ to download a free copy of the Geneva Bible and others. (Courtesy of A Puritan's Mind website.) Accessed April 24, 2018.
2. See http://www.champs-of-truth.com/reform/LUT_95TH.PDF to download a free copy of Martin Luther's "The 95 Theses." (Courtesy of Champs of Truth website.) Other websites also offer it free. Search "95 Theses" in your browser to find them. Accessed April 23, 2018.
3. "The 95 Theses," numbers 32, 35, and 36.
4. Britroyals, "King James I (1603–1625)," https://www.britroyals.com/kings.asp?id=james1. Accessed April 24, 2018.
5. Encyclopedia Britannica, "Hampton Court Conference," https://www.britannica.com /event/Hampton-Court-Conference. Accessed April 24, 2018.
6. *History Today*, Richard Cavendish, "Hampton Court Conference," http://www .historytoday.com/richard-cavendish/hampton-court-conference. First published in *History Today*, Volume 54, Issue 1, January 2004. Accessed online April 24, 2018.
7. StackExchange, "Christianity," https://christianity.stackexchange.com/questions/7082/why -arent-the-biblical-apocrypha-included-in-the-protestant-bible. Accessed April 24, 2018.
8. Bible Research, "The Old Testament Canon and Apocrypha," http://www.bible-researcher .com/canon2.html. Accessed April 24, 2018.
9. Sacred Texts, Apocrypha, Sirach, chapter 1, http://www.sacred-texts.com/bib/apo/sir001 .htm. Accessed April 24, 2018.
10. The e.Lib, The Apocrypha, http://wn.elib.com/Library/Religious/AP/Apocry_wisdm.html. Accessed April 24, 2018.
11. Bible Gateway, 1 Maccabees 1, New Revised Standard Version, "Alexander the Great," https://www.biblegateway.com/passage/?search=1+Maccabees+1&version=NRSV. Accessed April 24, 2018.
12. Bible Gateway, 2 Maccabees 1, New Revised Standard Version, "A Letter to the Jews in

Egypt," https://www.biblegateway.com/passage/?search=2+Maccabees+1&version=NRSV. Accessed April 24, 2018.

13. Encyclopedia Britannica, "Tobit," https://www.britannica.com/topic/Tobit-biblical -literature. Accessed April 24, 2018.

14. Bible Gateway, "Bel and the Dragon," New Revised Standard Version, https://www .biblegateway.com/passage/?search=Bel+and+the+Dragon&version=NRSV. Accessed April 24, 2018.

15. Bible History Daily, Robin Gallaher Branch, "Judith, a Remarkable Heroine," https://www .biblicalarchaeology.org/daily/people-cultures-in-the-bible/people-in-the-bible/judith-a -remarkable-heroine/, August 12, 2016. Accessed April 24, 2018.

16. Jewish Women's Archive, Encyclopedia, Carey A. Moore, "Esther: Apocrypha," https://jwa .org/encyclopedia/article/esther-apocrypha. Accessed April 24, 2018.

17. Jewish Encyclopedia, "Book of Baruch," Crawford Howell Toy, http://www .jewishencyclopedia.com/articles/2565-baruch-book-of. Accessed April 24, 2018.

18. Geneva Bible. See http://www.apuritansmind.com/free-geneva-bible-downloads-and -other-bibles/ to download a free copy of it and other bibles. (Courtesy of A Puritan's Mind website.) Accessed April 24, 2018.

CHAPTER 4

AUTHORING OF THE MAGNA CARTA

For the salvation of our soul.

—Magna Carta

T he thirteenth century didn't start well for the new King of England.

John Lackland, youngest son of Henry II and Eleanor of Aquitaine, had inherited the largest empire in Europe in 1199. At the dawn of the thirteenth century, all of England, Wales, Ireland, and most of France were under one regent, thanks, in part, to his predecessor, Richard the Lionheart.[1]

John, whose persona was depicted as the foil of the sixteenth-century ballad "A Gest of Robyn Hode,"[2] was considered by history as someone less than favorable to sit on the throne. After the death of his brother, the not-so-lion-hearted sibling of Richard ascended to rule England and began to conspire against everybody, including his two living brothers and their respective sons, especially Arthur (not that one), who claimed the crown to be his. John allegedly oversaw the murder of his nephew, and legend proposes that this royal villain depicted in the legendary tales of Robin Hood and his so-called "merry men" was a treacherous monarch, a corrupt tyrant, a weak leader in war, and the most despised regent in the history of England.[3]

Within five years of taking the throne, John had squandered the wealth of a nation, lost vital land holdings to France, found himself in a civil dispute with English barons over rights of landowners, had seen the territory of Normandy annexed by France, and had been kicked out of the Catholic Church under Pope Innocent III. While some historians would look back and describe John's reign as ruthless, his initiatives to begin building what would become one of the most formidable navies in the world, and his construction of the famous London Bridge, stand as two major historical feats attributed to the wicked king.

John is best remembered, however, for signing a document that would forever define the way that governments would consider the rights of those who were governed.

Following the catastrophic loss in a conflict between England and France, which plummeted Britain into near poverty, John sequestered himself in Windsor Castle as a means of survival. He was surrounded on all sides by twenty-five prominent landowners (known as "barons") who had seen enough self-pillaging of their respective countrysides for the pleasure of the crown that they rebelled.

Under siege and financial stress, the incompetent king was forced by his landowners, subjects, and church leaders to concede to growing demands for equal rights regarding a range of matters, including the assignment of troops, tariffs, taxes, labor fees, and basic human rights of the common folk. On June 15, 1215, a reluctant king was pressured by the strong influence of the barons, who held the city of London and the banks of the River Thames hostage, to enter into an agreement that has influenced civil liberties and constitutional rights of the people for more than eight hundred years.

The Magna Carta was based loosely on the ancient Anglo-Saxon law that was founded on the four basic freedoms: freedom of speech, freedom of worship, freedom from want or need, and freedom from oppression. It established the substance for incorporating these and other fundamental self-evident human rights into constitutions that have defined modern civilization (or at least tried to) for more than eight centuries. Consider the following from this inspired document:

> No free man shall be seized or imprisoned, or stripped of his rights or possessions, or outlawed or exiled, or deprived of his standing in any way, nor will we proceed with force against him, or send others to do so, except by the lawful judgment of his equals or by the law of the land. . . . To no one deny or delay right or justice.[4]

Reluctant to sign and agree to the document, John was not a fan of the idea that God's laws should be above his own. The Magna Carta ("Great Charter") is held to be one of the most significant documents of human history and even became part of the formation of writings adopted by America's forefathers. It influenced James Madison in his drafting of the Constitution of the United States[5] five hundred years later. The document, which is only survived by four originals, established the foundation of rules declaring everyone subject to the law (including the king), as well as guaranteeing the rights of individual justice and the right to a fair trial by one's peers.

Life, liberty, and property were core tenets of human rights protected by the Magna Carta,[6] but its origins are deeply rooted in the relationship between man and a higher king as its preface implies:

> Know that before God, for the health of our soul and those of our ancestors and heirs, to the honor of God, the exaltation of the holy Church, and the better ordering of our kingdom.

Further examination of the Magna Carta has suggested that it was published at the behest of the church[7] rather than just as a means of appeasing a potential civic disaster. Recent research conducted by Cambridge and King's College London has established further support that England had intended the Magna Carta to be distributed throughout Europe (in part because of the political infiltration of well-placed bishops as scribes who were charged with making copies for distribution) in an attempt to expand the church's locus of influence throughout Europe.

While the fact that the archbishop of Canterbury served as a liaison between the angry barons of England and their greedy king, historians further suggest that the document was also intended to serve as a contract between royalty and deity. The idea of keeping worldly kings under the continued scrutiny of heavenly hosts was nothing new by the thirteenth century. Some of the earliest scriptural writings regarding moral and civic justice and the relationship between God and kings abound in the Old Testament:

> Melchizedek king of Salem brought forth bread and wine: and he was the priest of the most high God. . . . He that justifieth the wicked, and he that condemneth the just, even they both are abomination to the Lord. . . . Judges and officers shalt thou make thee in all thy gates, which the Lord thy God giveth thee, throughout thy tribes: and they shall judge the people with just judgment. . . . Keep thee far from a false matter; and the innocent and righteous slay thou not: for I will not justify the wicked. (Genesis 14:18; Proverbs 17:15; Deuteronomy 16:18; Exodus 23:7)

The assertion of the Magna Carta's stand on supreme rule was predicated upon the notion that a higher law (God's commandments) was uncontestable and must be followed. Beyond the laws of Moses, and further ratified by Christ, origins of the implied message of the Magna Carta also abound in New Testament dialog, which foreshadows these fundamental principles of virtue in government and further establishes that a king is not the law itself but is subject to a higher law. In Romans chapter 8, we read,

> There is therefore now no condemnation to them which are in Christ Jesus, who walk not after the flesh, but after the Spirit. For the law of the Spirit of life in Christ Jesus hath made me free from the law of sin and death. For what the law could not do, in that it was weak through the flesh, God sending his own Son in the likeness of sinful flesh, and for sin, condemned sin in the flesh: That the righteousness of the law might be fulfilled in us, who walk not after the flesh, but after the Spirit. (Romans 8:1–4)

Stephen Langton, the archbishop who served as moderator and coauthor of the original document, considered the righteous rule of not only the nation's current population, but also its posterity when he admonished his regent to consider the liberties of his subjects inviolable (never to be broken, infringed, or dishonored). He wrote,

> John, by the grace of God, King of England . . . know ye, that we, in the presence of God and for the salvation of our soul and the souls of all our ancestors and heirs and unto the honour of God and the advancement of the Holy Church and amendment

of our realm . . . by this our present charter confirmed, for us and our heirs, forever; that the Church of England shall be free and have her whole rights and her liberties inviolable.[8] (Magna Carta)

The rights and freedoms of England were granted by the church as a result of interpreting the fundamental ideology of faith in Jesus Christ, as well as how New Testament laws and ordinances should be applied throughout English culture. Christian scholars have long claimed the Magna Carta as establishing a victory, not just for civil liberties, but for the support of a divinely inspired government as well. It has stood for almost a thousand years—in England, at least—and spawned the religious and civic liberties of the most independent and successful nations in the world: England, Canada, Australia, New Zealand, and the United States.

Now interpreted, intermingled, immortalized, deliberated, debated by democratic governments around the world, and inspired by the words of a cadre of oppressed as well as righteous stewards, the Magna Carta established the fundamental principles of "Life, Liberty, and the Pursuit of Happiness" and must be observed by all, regardless of station. Its origins are deeply rooted in human nature to accept government rule based on the precept that the psalmist declared twenty-five hundred years ago:

For the Lord most high is terrible; he is a great King over all the earth. . . . He ruleth by his power for ever; his eyes behold the nations. . . . O let the nations be glad and sing for joy: for thou shalt judge the people righteously, and govern the nations upon earth. . . . The Lord hath prepared his throne in the heavens; and his kingdom ruleth over all. (Psalms 47:2; 66:7; 67:4; and 103:19)

Notes

1. Encyclopedia Britannica, Geoffrey Wallis Steuart Barrow, "Richard I, King of England," https://www.britannica.com/biography/Richard-I-king-of-England, March 30, 2018. Accessed April 24, 2018.
2. Middle English Text Series, Robin Hood and Other Outlaw Tales, "A Gest of Robyn Hode," ed. Stephen Knight and Thomas H. Ohlgren (Rochester, NY: University of Rochester, 1997). See http://d.lib.rochester.edu/teams/text/gest-of-robyn-hode. Accessed April 24, 2018.
3. The Telegraph, Marc Morris, "King John: the most evil monarch in Britain's history," https://www.telegraph.co.uk/culture/11671441/King-John-the-most-evil-monarch-in-Britains-history.html, June 13, 2015. Accessed April 24, 2018.
4. See The British Library Treasures in Full, https://www.law.gmu.edu/assets/files/academics/founders/MagnaCarta.pdf to download a free copy of the Magna Carta. (Courtesy of The British Library Treasures in Full website.) Accessed April 24, 2018.

5. Library of Congress, "Magna Carta Muse and Mentor: Magna Carta and the US Constitution," https://www.loc.gov/exhibits/magna-carta-muse-and-mentor/magna-carta -and-the-us-constitution.html. Accessed on April 24, 2018.

6. CultureWatch, Bill Muehlenberg's commentary on issues of the day, "Magna Carta the Christian Connection," https://billmuehlenberg.com/2015/06/16/magna-carta-the -christian-connection/, June 16, 2015. Accessed April 24, 2018.

7. Independent, David Keys, "Magna Carta: New research sheds light on the church's role in publishing world-famous charter," https://www.independent.co.uk/news/uk/home-news /magna-carta-new-research-sheds-light-on-the-churchs-role-in-publishing-world-famous -charter-10318826.html, June 14, 2015. Accessed April 24, 2018.

8. See The British Library Treasures in Full.

CHAPTER 5

GREAT AWAKENING AND COLONIZATION OF AMERICA

Subject unto higher powers.

—Romans 13:1

B y the beginning of the seventeenth century, the Roman Catholic Church was the ruling body over most of the Christian world. Rome's influence, strengthened throughout Europe as a result of the deep historical influences of the nine Crusades for the Holy Land, would cement its strong religious hold on political heads of state throughout Europe, most of whom to this day remain distant relatives of one another.

But a new era of understanding, which focused on secular individuality and religious inspiration on the freedoms of worship, began to spread, largely spawned out of Martin Luther's disappointment with his Catholic leaders.

Under the scrutiny of James I, and later Charles I, oppressive rules regarding religious dissenters in Britain stirred the hearts and faith of a group of Puritans who chose to flee England. After their break with the Anglican Church, a group of English separatists turned their fealty to Amsterdam in hopes of starting new and independent lives. But Dutch life was difficult, and the work was hard for the English transplants. Concerned for their sense of identity as English folk among the Dutch, and possibly out of the growing tension between Holland and Spain, the settlers, led by Myles Standish and William Brewster, again boarded the now-famous vessel known as the *Mayflower* and set sail west for open water. They arrived in Plymouth Harbor in the New World after sixty-five days on the high seas of the Atlantic.

Though they had been navigating toward what they had hoped to be the newly established colony of Virginia, due to bad weather, the settlers landed in Massachusetts in Plymouth Harbor, setting in motion a chain of events that would transform an entire continent into a beacon of independent thought, religious freedom, and prosperity.

By the middle of the eighteenth century, American colonists began to migrate from Europe en masse to embrace new lands and new philosophies on prayer, baptism, and the role of religion in day-to-day life. The Church of England (led by the king himself rather than a Pope or Holy Roman Emperor) was not pleased with the influx of new religious ideas being propagated throughout America. Such caprices of thought, it was speculated, would lead to the potential for uprising and rebellion; the loss of assets, land holdings, and trade; and a wide range of new imports from the Colonies.

On the strength of influences such as those of Catholic evangelist Jonathan Edwards, who ministered to Massachusetts colonists in the mid-1700s (and who refused to be coerced into following his contemporaries into switching to Protestantism), a spiritual renewal ignited throughout New England and evolved into what historians have referred to as the "Great Awakening."[1]

Some historians suggest Edwards's doctrinal and theological prowess was fueled by his capacity to successfully recap the main principles of Puritanism and the Reformation and apply those ideologies to colonial life's daily pursuits. Edwards believed that personal conversion was predicated on an open confession of one's faith and acceptance of Jesus as Lord and Savior. Without such confession, parishioners were not worthy (or allowed) to take the sacraments of Communion. A student of John Calvin's teachings, Edwards was also concerned that God's children were spending too much time pursuing the things of the world rather than being humble and submissive before God. In his 1741 sermon "Sinners in the Hands of an Angry God," he taught,

> There is nothing that keeps wicked men at any one moment out of hell, but the mere pleasure of God. By the mere pleasure of God, I mean his sovereign pleasure, his arbitrary will, restrained by no obligation, hindered by no manner of difficulty, any more than if nothing else but God's mere will had in the least degree, or in any respect whatsoever, any hand in the preservation of wicked men one moment.[2]

In this same sermon, Edwards preached of a deity that was weary of the sins of men. He said, "All wicked men's pains and contrivance which they use to escape hell, while they continue to reject Christ, and so remain wicked men, do not secure them from hell one moment."

One of the fundamental arguments associated with Edwards's outcry against material expansion was linked to the rising level of interest and exploitation of the colonists by their king across the ocean. Authoritarian rule, it seemed, lost its luster when separated by three thousand miles of open sea. Further, given to mass assemblies by the general public and the colonists being so far away from royal oversight, argument over independent thought replaced the common courtesies of the gentry as a means of discussing how to better understand the nature of God and his relationship with an independent soul.

Christian sects began to separate themselves and form around various interpretations of Christian principles pertaining to the Holy Trinity, salvation, and the relationship between life, liberty, and property. Amidst the growing expansion of opinions about what to believe, how to worship changed as well, from orderly congregational gatherings into emotionally charged revivals. This spiritual rejuvenation, inspired by the music introduced by John and David Wesley, further changed the way colonial thought, philosophy, religion, and self-rule would evolve in the "New World."

The impact of the Great Awakening resulted in unifying a central philosophy that became the fuel that flamed the passion of politics and religion in eighteenth century America. Contrary to the status quo that supported the idea that the will of God was distributed by a regent or religious leader rang a hollow note to the rising number of individuals who discovered it was better to choose their respective paths for themselves. Removing the link between God and man, the head-of-state was reduced to little more than a peer of the people, which gave way to the notion that man share in self-governing but under the auspices of a Divine Creator.

Scholars of colonial history often suggest that the rapid spread of ideology relating to self-governance (rather than slavery, taxation, or tossing tea into a harbor) was the impetus that ignited the American Revolution and the outward rebellion against another king of England. Unlike the distant past in the time of King John and the barons of Britain, however, the colonial farmers and landowners, religious leaders, and common-ers no longer held their monarch accountable for the rising tide of tyranny across the land. Instead, they chose to do away with the monarchy altogether. Their assertion for religious, political, and economic independence from any worldly crown was still much rooted in their respective faith relating to the rule of law by a higher being. Thomas Jefferson wrote,

> When in the Course of human events it becomes necessary for one people to dissolve the political bands which have connected them with another and to assume among the powers of the earth, the separate and equal station to which the Laws of Nature and of Nature's God entitle them, a decent respect to the opinions of mankind re-quires that they should declare the causes which impel them to the separation. We hold these truths to be self-evident, that all men are created equal, that they are endowed by their Creator with certain unalienable Rights, that among these are Life, Liberty, and the pursuit of Happiness.[3] (Declaration of Independence)

The Great Awakening of the late eighteenth century and the subsequent revivalist period of the early half of the nineteenth century helped the various colonies that had taken up residence over hundreds of miles in remote and often savage regions of the frontier to unite under a common set of values and goals. A sense of community col-laboration emerged as a means of unifying common ideas around farming, trade, defense of liberties, and preservation of the core Christian value of self-sacrifice.[4]

Knowing that being subject to higher laws was inevitable, Paul wrote this concern-ing governance to the Christians of ancient Rome:

> Let every soul be subject unto the higher powers. For there is no power but of God: the powers that be are ordained of God. . . . For rulers are not a terror to good works,

but to the evil. Wilt thou then not be afraid of the power? Do that which is good, and thou shalt have praise of the same: For he is the minister of God to thee for good. But if thou do that which is evil, be afraid; for he beareth not the sword in vain: for he is the minister of God. (Romans 13:1, 3–4)

The early American settlers recognized the need for government, and they knew firsthand the consequences of being ruled by a monarchy. The colonists pursued a unified government almost immediately upon leaving their ships at Plymouth. This was evident by the formation of the Mayflower Compact.[5] Realizing that their lives and prosperity would need to be subject to some form of governance, they drafted and signed the Mayflower Compact to ensure a working community structure that would establish a rule of law that would align with God's.

The idea was that it would be an eternal king rather than an early regent. An eternal king who would inspire and establish those individuals to positions of authority based on his eternal plan, in the spirit that "Many are called but few are chosen."

NOTES

1. Encyclopedia Britannica, "Great Awakening: American Religious Movement," https://www.britannica.com/event/Great-Awakening. Accessed April 24, 2018.
2. Blue Letter Bible, Rev. Jonathan Edwards, "Sinners in the Hands of an Angry God," sermon preached at Enfield, July 8, 1741, https://www.blueletterbible.org/comm/edwards_jonathan/sermons/sinners.cfm. Accessed April 24, 2018.
3. US History.org, "The Declaration of Independence," http://www.ushistory.org/declaration/document/. Accessed April 24, 2018.
4. Bible Tools, "Bible Verses about Sacrifice as a Way of Life," https://www.bibletools.org/index.cfm/fuseaction/Topical.show/RTD/CGG/ID/5588/Sacrifice-as-Way-Life.htm. Accessed April 24, 2018.
5. Encyclopedia Britannica, "Mayflower Compact," https://www.britannica.com/topic/Mayflower-Compact. Accessed April 24, 2018.

CHAPTER 6

ESTABLISHMENT OF
THE UNITED STATES

A king shall reign in righteousness.

—Isaiah 32:1

The "Wonder of the world in this latter age for true happiness and felicity."[1]

These are among the closing words of the opening text in the authorized version of the Holy Bible, wishing high regard for the son of Mary, Queen of Scots.

While he was not without his own challenges and criticisms, few scholars in the Christian world would challenge the accomplishments of England's James I in his pursuit of unifying his Scottish Presbyterian faith with an inspired version of ancient scripture. His reputation as a royal peacemaker among his subjects (as well as between Catholic and Protestant sects) has been widely accepted by scholars[2] as nothing short of being a royal role model.

The Scottish king encouraged and financed the monumental task of standardizing the word of God into what has now become known as the King James Version of the Bible. He also undertook one of the most critically recognized experiments in the history of Western civilization: the independent colonization of the religious community known as Virginia on a continent more than three thousand miles away from the ruling masses of the British Crown.

Throughout the early sixteenth century, European explorers, including Spanish Jesuits, mapped the Chesapeake Bay. In 1583, England's "Virgin Queen" Elizabeth I approved Sir Walter Raleigh's quest to establish a "plantation" (meaning the creation of a community that would be "planted" in a foreign land) north of the Spanish territory known as Florida. His attempts to establish the territory, coined as "Virginia" in the queen's honor, ultimately failed and subsequently cost him his head at the strong urgency of the Spanish government[3] in 1618 in retaliation for a violation of the 1604 Treaty with Spain by members of his expedition.

As the new king of Scotland, Ireland, and England, in 1607, James I approved by royal charter the first establishment in the new Virginia Territory. The new settlement was named Jamestown in his honor. The objective, according to the Virginia Charter, was to establish a ruling community of "certain knights, gentlemen, merchants, and other adventurers"[4] by the grace of God. But the founding principles of the law of the land may have its roots better connected to the writings of a handful of Pilgrim pioneers rather than a Puritan prince.

Seeking refuge and freedom from James's Church of England, 41 religious separatists among the 102 passengers of the *Mayflower*[5] adopted the belief that since their ship had not landed at the English settlement of Virginia, but rather, in the unclaimed territory of Plymouth Harbor, their contract with the British crown and the Virginia Trading Company was void. Nonetheless, the settlers knew the risk and potential detriment of establishing a community without rule of law, and they entered into an agreement known as the Mayflower Compact, which states the following:

> In the name of God, Amen. We whose names are underwritten, the loyal subjects of our dread Sovereign Lord King James, by the Grace of God of Great Britain, France, and Ireland King, Defender of the Faith, etc. Having undertaken for the Glory of God and advancement of the Christian Faith and Honour of our King and Country, a Voyage to plant the First Colony in the Northern Parts of Virginia, do by these presents solemnly and mutually in the presence of God and one of another, Covenant and Combine ourselves together in a Civil Body Politic, for our better ordering and preservation and furtherance of the ends aforesaid; and by virtue hereof to enact, constitute and frame such just and equal Laws, Ordinances, Acts, Constitutions and Offices from time to time, as shall be thought most meet and convenient for the general good of the Colony, unto which we promise all due submission and obedience. In witness whereof we have hereunder subscribed our names at Cape Cod, the 11th of November, in the year of the reign of our Sovereign Lord King James, of England, France and Ireland the eighteenth, and of Scotland the fifty-fourth. Anno Domini 1620.[6]

The Pilgrims recognized the need for the rule of law to govern effectively throughout a range of ideologies if they were going to make their new colony survive—let alone prosper—while maintaining a close connection with the will of righteous governance. While the author of the Mayflower Compact is uncertain, likely candidates were the educated William Brewster and John Carver, who were among the forty-one men who signed and agreed to the charter for governing the new immigrants. Given their fealty to the Crown, the colonists agreed by virtue of the Compact that four core tenets would provide the guidelines for governance. They are as follows:

1. They would remain faithful to the British Crown.

2. They would live in accordance with Christian principles.
3. They would establish a single frame of community and agree to work together to build it.
4. The colonists would establish and abide by "laws, ordinances, acts, constitutions, and offices" to benefit the fledgling colony.

Electing Carver as the governor over the Plymouth Colony in 1620, the group settled for the winter with only half of them surviving into 1621. By spring, their first governor and half the population of the Plymouth Colony had perished, leaving the rest to elect William Bradford as the new governor, to continue to govern based on what John Quincy Adams once referred to as "the original social compact" and further establish the fundamental tenets of self-governance in the New World.

Fast-forward one hundred years, through four major wars and countless skirmishes between settlers and natives, and the Colonies of America were ripe for independence.

Over the course of the seventeenth and first half of the eighteenth centuries, the colonies had developed into a lucrative source of commerce for England. They had also inspired controversy. The region known as New England was under great scrutiny by Britain, France, the native populations who felt encroached upon, and the colonists themselves who had aspirations for expansion.

Then came the Great Awakening of 1730, which saw the rapid spread of evangelical Christianity reshape the nature of colonial ideology toward independence and away from their British overseers. Following the Boston Massacre in 1770, when British soldiers shot into a mob of angry citizens, killing five of the assembled rioters, the colonists soon formed their own loosely held government of colonial representation as part of their growing disdain for the way the Crown had treated the rights of the American colonists.

The Americans of the thirteen colonies united against a new system of royal taxation in the form of the Stamp Act of 1765. Between 1766 and 1774, colonists initiated a series of coordinated resistance to the onslaught of new royal actions by following civic protocols, establishing committees, and exchanging ideas between colonists rather than through the establishment of a united political faction.

The Continental Congress of 1774, organized by Thomas Jefferson, Patrick Henry, and Peyton Randolph, requested delegates from twelve of the thirteen designated territories throughout New England. They were to assemble in Philadelphia and discuss possible courses of action in response to colonial protests against the Crown. Absent were delegates from Georgia, which was embroiled in a British-funded conflict with the Creek Indians (although the colony would later appoint Benjamin Franklin as colonial delegate).

With James long since being succeeded by twelve British regents, his dream of a spiritual outpost in the New World had become larger than a dozen subsequent monarchs could contain. Foreshadowing what would become some of the most sacred words of American doctrine, and echoing tenets from the Magna Carta, the Declaration and

Resolves of the First Continental Congress[7] affirmed that "they are entitled to life, liberty, and property, and they have never ceded to any sovereign power whatever a right to dispose of either without their consent."

Twenty years before he helped lay the foundation of what would be established as the United States of America, John Adams posited that a nation would do well to prosper under the singular, supernal direction of the Bible as a means of government. In his diary he wrote,

> Suppose a nation in some distant region should take the Bible as their only law book and every member should regulate his conduct by the precepts there exhibited. Every member would be obligated in conscience to temperance and frugality and industry, to justice and kindness and charity toward his fellowmen, and to piety, love, and reverence toward Almighty God. . . . No man would steal or lie or in any way defraud his neighbor but would live in peace and good will toward all men. No man would blaspheme his Maker or profane his worship, but a rational and manly, a sincere and unaffected devotion would reign in the hearts of all men. What a utopia, what a paradise this region would be![8]

On July 4, 1776, representing more than two million American citizens, fifty-six men assembled to sign a document that would dedicate and sanctify a nation—for better or worse—to the preservation of a way of life that was predicated on the principles alluded to by the Prophet Isaiah:

> Behold, a king shall reign in righteousness, and princes shall rule in judgment. And a man shall be as an hiding place from the wind, and a covert from the tempest; as rivers of water in a dry place, as the shadow of a great rock in a weary land. And the eyes of them that see shall not be dim, and the ears of them that hear shall hearken. (Isaiah 32:1–3)

NOTES

1. King James Version of the Bible, The Epistle Dedicatory, iii.
2. The Tudor Society, Heather R. Darsie, "James I and VI: Tudor King," https://www.tudorsociety.com/james-i-vi-tudor-king-heather-r-darsie/. Accessed April 24, 2018.
3. History.org, Colonial Williamsburg, Bruce P. Lenman, "Virginia's Father, King James I," http://www.history.org/foundation/journal/autumn01/jamesi.cfm. Accessed April 24, 2018.
4. American History, "The First Virginia Charter 1606," http://www.let.rug.nl/usa/documents/1600-1650/the-first-virginia-charter-1606.php. Accessed April 24, 2018.
5. Plimoth Plantation, "Mayflower and Mayflower Compact," http://www.plimoth.org/learn/just-kids/homework-help/mayflower-and-mayflower-compact. Accessed April 24, 2018.
6. Ibid.

7. Yale Law School, Lillian Goldman Law Library, The Avalon Project, "Declaration and Resolves of the First Continental Congress," http://avalon.law.yale.edu/18th_century/resolves.asp. Accessed April 24, 2018.

8. John Quincy Adams diary, February 22, 1756. See Christian Defense Fund, One Nation under God, "John Adams," http://www.leaderu.com/orgs/cdf/onug/jadams.html. Accessed April 24, 2018.

PART II

RESTORING CHRISTIAN FUNDAMENTALS

───────── ❧ ─────────

Ecce tabernaculum Dei cum hominibus!

Behold, the dwelling place of God is with man! (Revelation 21:3)

Foreshadowing the inevitable . . .

This section explores six historical events that may suggest we are all part of a bigger plan than many might either acknowledge or hope for. (Although for some, given the conditions of our world, it's a welcome notion that there might be any plan at all!)

When looking after the disposition of mankind, for more than two thousand years, legend, prophecies, oracles, and even astronomers have deliberated on the notion that the clock is winding down on mortality. As discussed in chapter 1, in religious studies, the eschatology[1] of the human race is the study of the life, disposition, death, and judgment of man.

For early Christians, the *Epiphany*, or *epiphanaeia*,[2] represented the return of Christ in his glory, while Judaism contends that the whole idea of a Second Coming is little more than a ruse contrived by dissatisfied Christians (and displaced Jews). Why couldn't Jesus, they argue, get what he needed done during his mortal ministry (including saving them from the Romans)?

When will the End of Days actually occur? In his second letter to Timothy, Paul warns of a "perilous" time in the last days when men will be "without natural affection . . . disobedient to parents" and "despisers of those that are good."

Some scholars suggest the end has already begun, and if current affairs in the Middle East (or even closer to home) are any indication that humanity is running out of time, references by early Church leaders shortly after the death of Christ suggest the eschatology of man might be more predictable than most people think.

Christianity teaches that there will be a reckoning of souls upon the closing days of man on the earth, meaning that the righteous will be united with Jesus at his coming, being spared God's angry wrath upon the world, while there will be "hell to pay" for those who have chosen wickedness as a way of life. As was also previously discussed, although many cultures throughout history claimed to know when the Lord will return, the scriptures record that even Christ himself does not know the day that God will send him back to us.

Now, almost two thousand years since Jesus's departure, the Christian world still looks to the day when Jesus will return. We live in a time when the men Paul wrote of seem to walk among us en masse:

> Men shall be lovers of their own selves, covetous, boasters, proud, blasphemers, disobedient to parents, unthankful, unholy, without natural affection, trucebreakers, false accusers, incontinent, fierce, despisers of those that are good, traitors, heady, highminded, lovers of pleasures more than lovers of God; having a form of godliness, but denying the power thereof: from such turn away. (2 Timothy 3:2–5)

NOTES

1. Encyclopedia Britannica, Richard Landes, "Eschatology," https://www.britannica.com/topic/eschatology. Accessed April 24, 2018.
2. Plainer Words, Tom L. Ballinger, "Epiphaneia," http://www.plainerwords.com/artman2/publish/2007/Epiphaneia.shtml, February 26, 2008. Accessed April 24, 2018.

CHAPTER 7

KING JAMES'S VERSION OF THE TYNDALE-VULGATE BIBLE

To them that walk in darkness.[1]

"Vulgar."

Most of the European bluebloods of the early sixteenth century viewed any attempt at an English translation of the Latin Bible, also known as the "Vulgate," as something akin to being unsuitable and downright blasphemous. In the 1500s, a common English translation of anything this side of Homer, Plato, or Socrates was considered less than favorable—especially the word of God.

Some might find it ironic as well that the term's origins "to make common" (which Jerome was attempting to do with his thirteenth-century Latin translation of the Bible) appeared to be in opposition to the idea that God's word was for the general masses, as well as for those actually conducting the Mass.

Another idea is that God's teachings were meant only for those people (men) who were authorized to lead the church of the times, contrary to what was found in 1 Kings 2:3–4. It reads,

> Keep the charge of the Lord your God, to walk in his ways, to keep his statutes, his commandments, his ordinances, and his testimonies, according to what is written in the Law of Moses, that you may succeed in all that you do and wherever you turn, so that the Lord may carry out his promise which he spoke concerning me, saying, if your sons are careful of their way, to walk before me in truth with all their heart and with all their soul, you shall not lack a man on the throne of Israel.

For more than a millennium, only Rome itself could dictate and interpret the words of Moses, Christ, and his Apostles, which had been locked away in Hebrew, Greek, and Latin translations and made available for public readings only by church leadership.

Many scholars of the day started asking questions, not only about the limited access to the scriptures but also of the real intent of the church in keeping commoners from gaining a better understanding of what was in the writings considered "doctrine." How could God's faithful "keep his statutes" and "walk in his ways" as it was written if they couldn't read, study, ponder, and fully comprehend what he was telling them to do?

You don't have to look any further than in the accounts of the religious bias of the day and how protective the church leaders were of their sacred texts (or of the many frivolous taxes and fees they imposed on their faithful—and often gullible—congregations). Aside from early translations by Wycliffe and Erasmus, both of which were seen as more experimental than holy writ, the local leaders (religious as well as civil) didn't take too well to anybody, scholarly or otherwise, interpreting the Bible (and, consequently, gaining a better understanding of its content) in the common tongue of the people.

Along comes young William Tyndale, a twenty-six-year-old second-year student at Oxford University who showed great passion for the common man (and maybe just a dash of hubris), mixed with a generous dose of being one's "brother's keeper." A student of Erasmus, Tyndale was convinced that the word of God needed to be found as familiar with the farmer in the field as it was with the parish priest. He declared, "If God spare my life, ere many years pass, I will cause a boy that driveth the plow shall know more of the Scripture than [the clergy] dost."[2]

Religious curiosity, independent thought, higher learning, and mass communications converged in Europe in the early 1500s. Johannes Gutenberg's new development in mass printing provided an affordable means of making the written word available in mass quantities. Martin Luther's freshly translated German version of the Bible, along with his subsequent ninety-five points of concern against the Catholic Church,[3] became the period's version of a best seller and is considered by historians to be the tipping point for triggering the Reformation and launching the Protestant movement.

Tyndale, influenced by Luther and a lifelong student of the Bible, took issue with the Vulgate translations as being too complex. He took specific umbrage with the fact that most of the priests couldn't even read Latin!

He wrote that the word of God was "the basis of salvation and the grace of God its essence." The church considered his perspectives on the Roman belief of the "written word" as heresy (primarily because Tyndale challenged the dishonesty and arrogance of the priests). Tyndale's translation of the Greek and German scriptures into the common English tongue suggested his driving desire to reveal what he perceived as open corruption among the ranks of the clergy as much as it was from his sense of public virtue. The church controlled all aspects of religious education and charged churchgoers for everything. He was open with his accusations and declared,

> What a trade is that of the priests. They want money for everything: money for baptism, money for churchings, for weddings, for buryings, for images, brotherhoods, penances, soul-masses, bells, organs, chalices, copes, surplices, ewers, censors, and all manner of ornaments. Poor sheep! The parson shears, the vicar shaves, the parish priest polls, the friar scrapes, the indulgence seller pares . . . all that you want is a

butcher to flay you and take away your skin. He will not leave you long. Why are your prelates dressed in red? Because they are ready to shed the blood of whomsoever seeketh the word of God? Scourge of states, devastators of kingdoms, the priests take away not only Holy Scripture, but also prosperity and peace; but of their councils is no layman; reigning over all, they obey nobody; and making all concur to their own greatness, they conspire against every kingdom.[4]

But mid-sixteenth-century England wasn't comfortable with the idea that an upstart from Gloucester could possibly have the sense of the ages to take the lead in translating the Bible for the common folk. As a result, Tyndale left Cambridge for more hospitable conditions in Germany, the center of Lutheran thought, where, in 1525, he translated the Greek New Testament into English and forever linked the messages of the Messiah with what he described as "the word of thy soul's health."

Tyndale, who spoke and wrote in the six "romantic" languages, was a master of English and spent the rest of his life in Germany and Belgium translating and publishing his English version of the New Testament. In the company of close friends, who leaned toward the new Lutheran way of looking at reforming the powerful hold the Catholic leaders had on their flocks, Tyndale wrote the following in his prologue of the 1525 translation:

For who is so blind to ask why light should be shewed to them that walk in darkness, where they cannot but stumble, and where to stumble is the danger of eternal damnation.[5]

Center to that hold was the interpretation of God's word.

To Tyndale's credit (as well as his ultimate peril), his work on translating the New Testament, and shortly afterward his translation of the Pentateuch (with the assistance of Miles Coverdale), ultimately cost the forty-two-year-old scholar his life. Tyndale's efforts, however, resulted in fifteen thousand copies of scripture (in "vulgar English") being distributed to rich and poor alike and further inspired Coverdale to take up the cause "with the King's most gracious license" to produce what became the first authorized "standard works" in English.

William Tyndale's work and Coverdale's subsequent complete manuscript of the Protestant Bible in English (with the Catholic Apocrypha as an appendix) gave way to what would become the "Great Bible" and, ultimately, the foundation on which the Hampton Court Conference of 1604 would base their revisions to produce King James's authorized version in 1611. The Bible, which has become the most printed book in the history of mankind, fulfills the commandment given by the Savior as written in the book of Mark to "Go ye into all the world, and preach the gospel to every creature. He that believeth and is baptized shall be saved; but he that believeth not shall be damned" (Mark 16:15–16).

Tyndale was executed in Antwerp in 1535 for the charge of "corrupting God's holy word," but his ultimate judgment by his peers was left to the ages. He is commonly revered as "The Apostle of England"[6] and the forefather to the Bible in English for the world. Were it not for his work, as well as that of his student Coverdale's that followed, the King James Bible might have been interpreted far differently. With his dying prayer, "Lord, open the King of England's eyes," Tyndale died not knowing that Henry VIII had already sanctioned the printing of his version of the Bible for the masses.

Four hundred years later, and just as Paul declared in Ephesians (unlocked by Tyndale for the world to discover), Tyndale's passion, as well as his peril, laid the groundwork for what some would consider God's final chapter for mankind: "In the dispensation of the fulness of times he [will] gather together in one all things in Christ, both which are in heaven, and which are on earth" (Ephesians 1:10).

Notes

1. Prologue of William Tyndale's 1525 translation of the Bible. See FaithofGod.net, "Prologues to the New Testament," http://faithofgod.net/TyNT/Prologue.htm. Accessed April 24, 2018.
2. *Christianity Today*, Tony Lane, "A Man for All People: Introducing William Tyndale," https://www.christianitytoday.com/history/issues/issue-16/man-for-all-people-introducing-william-tyndale.html. Accessed April 24, 2018.
3. Encyclopedia Britannica, "Ninety-Five Theses," https://www.britannica.com/event/Ninety-five-Theses. Accessed April 24, 2018.
4. J. H. Merle d'Aubigné, History of the Great Reformation of the Sixteenth Century, vol. 5, translated by H. White (New York: Robert Carter and Brothers, 1853), 214–15.
5. Prologue, Tyndale's 1525 translation of the Bible.
6. Free Reformed Churches, Reverend Laurens Roth, "William Tyndale: The Apostle to England, 1490?–1536," http://frcna.org/publications/item/8641. Accessed April 24, 2018.

CHAPTER 8

ESTABLISHMENT OF THE U.S. CONSTITUTION

Righteousness exalteth a nation.

—Proverbs 14:34

Does God appear in the Constitution?

Not from a literal standpoint, although references to God or the divine is incorporated into all fifty states' constitutions. So why not in the big document?

Following the success of the American Revolution, the Constitutional Convention, which was established among the thirteen original colonies, convened in Philadelphia to deliberate over the final version of the charter that would serve as the guidepost for governing the new nation. A significant challenge among the colonies was how to agree on surrendering their respective sovereignty for a single form of leadership that would rule over so many different cultures, communities, faiths, and philosophies. The year before he was elected the nation's first president, George Washington wrote that the establishment of a government and its new constitution was nothing short of a miracle. He said,

> It appears to me, then, little short of a miracle, that the delegates from so many different states (which states you know are also different from each other in their manners, circumstances, and prejudices) should unite in forming a system of national government, so little liable to well-founded objections.[1]

To better understand what some historians consider having been spiritual and religious influences in the architecture and writing of the U.S. Constitution, a good place to start is in the words of the men who wrote it. Thomas Jefferson, who history notes as the "Father of the Declaration of Independence," believed that there was a place for God at the head of the national conscience, but in the sense that the relationship was personal, intimate, and free of political oversight. Jefferson stated,

> Believing with you that religion is a matter which lies solely between man and his God, that he owes account to none other for his faith or his worship, that the legislative powers of government reach actions only, and not opinions, I contemplate with sovereign reverence that act of the whole American people which declared that their legislature should "make no law respecting an establishment of religion, or prohibiting the free exercise thereof," thus building a wall of separation between church and State.[2]

Turning, then, to what inspired the hands of the men who authored the sacred document that stands as the cornerstone of the most powerful nation in the history of the world, the Founding Fathers understood the necessity of keeping God in the government, while also keeping the government out of the church. Prompted by the ambitions of James Madison and Alexander Hamilton to establish a central form of legislation and governance, John Adams believed the collective works of his and his colleagues was divinely inspired for the purpose of improving on the established "League of Friendship,"[3] which was enacted during the 1781 Articles of Confederation as a means of formally protecting the liberties of the people rather than limiting them. In one of many of his letters to his beloved Abigail, John Adams wrote,

> A Constitution of Government once changed from freedom can never be restored. Liberty, once lost, is lost forever. . . . Our Constitution was made only for a moral and religious people. It is wholly inadequate to the government of any other.[4]

In a classic example of walking the talk following the outcry for justice for the British soldiers who killed five rioters of the 1770 Boston Massacre, Adams took up the task of representing the soldiers in their trial[5] (reportedly for little more reason than because it was the right thing to do). As a matter of defense, Adams pointed to those rioters, who were equally accountable in the outcome, and stated that the defendants were merely responding to the potential threat of further hostilities by an angry mob descending upon them. Justice, like God, was no respecter of persons and was blind to the color of one's uniform. (It *would* be for Adams!)

Barely out of his teens when he graduated from Harvard University, Adams represented Massachusetts at the First Continental Congress in 1774, where he became close friends with future political rival Thomas Jefferson. Adams, Jefferson, and Washington, who have since been immortalized as three of the pillars of leadership throughout the transition of the Continental States into a fledgling nation, would each eventually serve as its president, even when many of the American masses would have settled for one of them to be crowned their king.[6]

Along with Hamilton, Washington, Madison, Adams, and Jefferson, Benjamin

Franklin would join the cadre of fifty-five men and would complete, seal, and ratify the Constitution of the new United States of America, which would stand as the governing document for the 3.5 million citizens then, and for more than 327 million citizens[7] today. Those immortal words read,

> We the People of the United States, in Order to form a more perfect Union, establish Justice, insure domestic Tranquility, provide for the common defence, promote the general Welfare, and secure the Blessings of Liberty to ourselves and our Posterity, do ordain and establish this Constitution for the United States of America.[8] (Preamble of the Constitution)

While James Madison is noted as the Father of the Constitution, it was Franklin who suggested that the document was sacred and inspired by a Divine Creator. History holds the inventor-statesman as a major figure and key influence in the creation of the tapestry that would become the fabric of American government. Of all the founders, Franklin is the only man who signed all four of the principal documents and treaties that gave the United States its status as a nation: the Declaration of Independence, the Constitution, the Treaty of Paris, and the Treaty of Alliance. To Benjamin Franklin, however, he was just a small figure granted providence to participate in establishing a bulwark based on the architecture designed by the will of a higher being. In an address on prayer, delivered in 1787, he stated,

> The longer I live, the more convincing proofs I see of this truth, that God governs in the affairs of men. And if a sparrow cannot fall to the ground without His notice, is it probable that an empire can rise without His aid? . . . If it had not been for the justice of our cause, and the consequent interposition of Providence, in which we had faith, we must have been ruined. If I had ever before been an atheist, I should now have been convinced of the being and government of a Deity![9]

In forming the foundation for the Republic, the fifty-five delegates met in secret over the course of seven weeks. They debated pertinent issues, such as the size of states, equal representation, whether or not to accept a regent as ruler, and slavery. In the end, the Connecticut or "Great Compromise"[10] was established, and through it came the product of equal representation through two governing houses in a process called "bi-cameral legislation."

The notion that God works to inspire the progression of some eternal plan was established early in the Bible in accounts throughout the Old and New Testaments, with special emphasis in the writings of the ancient prophet Isaiah. In Isaiah we read,

> And the government shall be upon his shoulder. . . . Of the increase of his government and peace there shall be no end, upon the throne of David, and upon his kingdom, to order it, and to establish it with judgment and with justice from henceforth even for ever. The zeal of the Lord of hosts will perform this. . . . For the Lord is our judge, the Lord is our lawgiver, the Lord is our king; he will save us. (Isaiah 9:6–7; 33:22)

Whether Isaiah was referring to the model of bicameral legislation when he referenced the Lord as a "judge," "lawgiver," and "king" is left for others to decide, but Franklin's inferences regarding divine providence suggest that the Founding Fathers might have been inspired by the three distinct references to the Lord, representing three branches of leadership in harmony to rule in righteousness. In the words of Benjamin Franklin:

> I must own I have so much faith in the general government of the world by Providence that I can hardly conceive a transaction of such momentous importance to the welfare of millions now existing, and to exist in the posterity of a great nation, should be suffered to pass without being in some degree influenced, guided, and governed by that omnipotent, omnipresent, and beneficent Ruler.[11]

Though the two founding documents of American history are the Declaration of Independence and the Constitution, the Declaration, which acknowledges "God" four times, establishes the rights of human beings as being granted by our Creator. The Constitution, however, which never mentions God, only implies divine right based on how we are to be governed. Although it was Madison who suggested that self-governance by the people, of the people, and for the people was predicated upon a certain amount of "sufficient virtue among men," ancient scripture suggests the success of a nation depends upon its righteous intent. In Proverbs we read, "Righteousness exalteth a nation: but sin is a reproach to any people" (Proverbs 14:34).

Ratified by America's second president, the righteous leadership of the Founding Fathers, with respect to the Constitution and the revolution that preceded its adoption, was echoed by John Adams when he said,

> Our Constitution was made only for a moral and religious people. It is wholly inadequate to the government of any other. . . . The highest glory of the American Revolution was this: it connected, in one indissoluble bond, the principles of civil government with the principles of Christianity.[12]

While those who assert that the United States was never envisioned to be a "Christian-centered" nation given the absence of "God" in the words of the Constitution, its principal author bore his own witness of being a man among those who became "fervent advocates in the cause of Christ." Echoing in faith and in his words in his letter to his dear friend and one-time political opponent Thomas Jefferson, John Adams encapsulated his vision for what has become a nation of agency, free ideas, and faith. He wrote,

> Suppose a nation in some distant region should take the Bible for their only law book, and every member should regulate his conduct by the precepts there exhibited! Every member would be obliged in conscience, to temperance, frugality, and industry; to justice, kindness, and charity toward his fellow men; and to piety, love and reverence toward Almighty God. . . . What a Utopia, what a Paradise would this region be.[13]

NOTES

1. National Archives, Founders Online, "From George Washington to Lafayette, 7 February 1788," https://founders.archives.gov/documents/Washington/04-06-02-0079. Accessed April 24, 2018.
2. Library of Congress Information Bulletin, "Jefferson's Letter to the Danbury Baptists," The Final Letter, as Sent, https://www.loc.gov/loc/lcib/9806/danpre.html. Accessed April 24, 2018.
3. The Gilder Lehrman Institute of American History, History Now, The Articles of Confederation, 1777, https://www.gilderlehrman.org/content/articles-confederation-1777. Accessed April 24, 2018.
4. National Archives, Founders Online, "John Adams to Abigail Adams, 7 July 1775," https://founders.archives.gov/documents/Adams/04-01-02-0160. Accessed April 24, 2018.
5. Biography, "John Adams Biography, U.S. President (1735–1826)," https://www.biography.com/people/john-adams-37967. Accessed April 24, 2018.
6. Vision.org, Wilf Hey, "George Washington: The Man Who Would Not Be King," http://www.vision.org/visionmedia/biography-george-washington/587.aspx. Accessed April 24, 2018.
7. United States Census Bureau, U.S. and World Population Clock, https://www.census.gov/popclock/. Accessed April 24, 2018.
8. To download a free copy of the Constitution, see https://www.usconstitution.net/const.pdf. Accessed April 24, 2018.
9. American Rhetoric, Online Speech Bank, Benjamin Franklin, Constitutional Convention Address on Prayer, delivered Thursday, June 28, 1787, Philadelphia, PA, http://www.americanrhetoric.com/speeches/benfranklin.htm. Accessed April 24, 2018.
10. World Atlas, "What Was the Great Compromise?" https://www.worldatlas.com/articles/what-was-the-great-compromise.html. Accessed April 24, 2018.
11. Anxious Bench, Thomas Kidd, "The Constitution 'Divinely Inspired'? Ben Franklin Answers," http://www.patheos.com/blogs/anxiousbench/2016/02/the-constitution-divinely-inspired-ben-franklin-answers/, February 23, 2016. Accessed April 24, 2018.
12. National Archives, Founders Online, "From John Adams to Massachusetts Militia, 11 October 1798," https://founders.archives.gov/documents/Adams/99-02-02-3102. Accessed April 24, 2018.
13. Google Books, Congressional Record, V. 146, Pt. 10, July 10, 2000, to July 17, 2000, https://books.google.com. Accessed April 24, 2018.

CHAPTER 9

REVELATION OF
THE BOOK OF MORMON

An ensign for the nations.

—Isaiah 11:12

"In the beginning."

Three words that foster all sorts of emotions, ranging from inspiration to anxiety.

From a unified concept among three of the most popular faiths on earth (Christianity, Judaism, and Islam) that God created the universe and everything in it out of nothing, "in the beginning" is a core precept. But the idea did not originate with the earliest writings of holy writ. The notion of "something from nothing" as part of the common thread among the three religions was a product of social evolution from the period following extensive political interpretations of the writings of the priestly authors of Genesis[1] during the fourth century.

Given that historians and scholars have surmised that there are multiple sources of authorship comprising the final published version of the book of Genesis, the ancient writings that were ultimately collected and published as Christian scripture are replete with symbolism, myth, analogy (also known as "parables"), and gems of historical intersections.[2]

Scholars also reveal through patterns identified that the ancient tomes held as sacred can be loosely cataloged into four basic categories. They are

1. Business affairs (Epistles)—The typical epistle, as those found in the writings of the New Testament. Apostle Paul provided "official" directives to the various Church branches throughout the empire for how the body of the Church should

operate in consistency regardless of location or political persuasion. These epistles became critical to further establishing the day-to-day operations in extending the Christian agenda throughout the Mediterranean regions and beyond.

2. Chronological events—These include accounts such as those in Exodus and Numbers and the books of the lesser prophets.

3. Witnesses—Provided as first-hand testimonials by prophets and apostles (and a few women whose voices were counted as well). The key differentiator is that their accounts testify of the divinity of Jesus (or Jehovah). Such witnesses appear in Isaiah in the Old Testament, along with the songs and psalms of David and Solomon and the traditional Gospels of Matthew, Mark, Luke, and John in the New Testament. Other witnesses appear throughout the Bible.

4. Commandments—Reference to this category extends beyond the Ten Commandments in Exodus 34 and consists of the many passages of legal guidelines found throughout the Old and New Testaments, including Leviticus and Deuteronomy and the accounts of Jesus's teachings (especially his Beatitudes) as documented in the New Testament Gospels.

These four elements of divine writing have always provided the necessary balance of direction, rebuke, and inspiration for man to live life under the watchful eye of the Creator. Foreshadowing of things to come and prophesying of events are also essential to Christian thought, and the Bible includes numerous passages of scripture that contain prophecies of events—some of which have already come to pass—and further revelation of thought, direction, and scripture.

John Calvin,[3] a sixteenth-century Protestant reformer and apologist, challenged the fundamental precepts of Christian doctrine and believed the idea that scripture was something akin to a spiritual education inspired by God (whatever form it may be revealed). He wrote,

> Scripture is the school of the Holy Spirit, in which, as nothing is omitted that is both necessary and useful to know, so nothing is taught but what is expedient to know. Therefore we must guard against depriving believers of anything disclosed about predestination in Scripture, lest we seem either wickedly to defraud them of the blessing of their God or to accuse and scoff at the Holy Spirit for having published what it is in any way profitable to suppress.[4]

The collection of sixty-six books found in the traditional Bible is considered by most Christians as definitive.[5] Some Christian sects, however, contend that God had much more to say than what the Scottish king and his Hampton Court Councils determined as being the complete works and words of God to all of his children.

A compelling characteristic of some Christian groups, however, including Mormonism, lies in the notion that God still talks to his children and that the collection of text assembled in the Holy Bible is only a fragment of scripture that represents the word and work of God. By contrast, for many in the Christian public, the idea that the word of God continues to be revealed is as difficult to believe as it is for the LDS faithful to believe that God no longer speaks to his children.

From a profound sense that there was more to the story of Christ and his Church than what the Councils at Nicaea and Hampton provided to the world, a tenet of Mormonism falls in line with the knowledge that Jesus had a larger influence on the world than just in the southern Mediterranean region of the Roman Empire. In John chapter 10, the Lord tells the Jews, "And other sheep I have, which are not of this fold: them also I must bring, and they shall hear my voice; and there shall be one fold, and one shepherd" (John 10:16).

Many Christian scholars suggest the reference Jesus made to "sheep" from another fold referred to his need to minister (by proxy) to the Gentiles of other lands[6] and to help convert the false prophets throughout the land of Israel—namely the Pharisees. LDS scholars, however, look to the east for the location of the "other sheep" as being those people who immigrated to the lands of what is now South and Central America. As with any culture, this group of migrating tribes brought their own records, which Mormonism claims to be "Another Testament of Jesus Christ."[7]

Further to the concept of Mormonism is the notion that the principles of revelation given to man by God through a holy order has not changed, although it was suspended from the world for almost two millennia and once re-established. It would again reveal many things by his authorized mouthpiece, as was foreseen by Isaiah. In the Old Testament we read,

> The earth shall be full of the knowledge of the Lord, as the waters cover the sea . . . The Lord shall set his hand again the second time to recover the remnant of his people, which shall be left. . . . And he shall set up an ensign for the nations, and shall assemble the outcasts of Israel, and gather together the dispersed of Judah from the four corners of the earth. (Isaiah 11:9, 11–12)

Foreknowledge of the Lord's return includes the posit that God still talks to the human race, which often forces people to question their own understanding of what they believe scripture to be.

Throughout history, ruling nations have had to dictate to their subjects how they should worship God and what may and may not be accepted as holy writ. About the time of the death and banishment of the last Apostles of Jesus, probably in response to the spread of Christianity throughout the Roman culture (though still heavily persecuted by the Pharisees and the Roman government), Jewish leaders held their own council at Jamnia[8] in the ancient town of Joppa to discuss what would become the revised authorized canon. In fact, history has shown numerous incidents when writings from the time of Jesus and before have been considered on-again, off-again doctrines of faith.

Although "scripture" in the LDS religion is defined as doctrine that may be inspired, revealed, or directed by the Holy Ghost and ratified by authorized Church leaders, the definition of what is considered "canon" is used to describe the sacred text considered standard works. The standard works encompass the Old and New Testaments, as well as the additional volume of the Book of Mormon, which the LDS people believe to be another record of the Lord's ministry in the Americas.

Scholars often study and attempt to validate and justify the evolutionary aspects of Christian canon. For Christianity in general, it's sufficient to get through a good portion of the Bible on a regular basis. For the Mormons, however, who consider "scripture" to include works beyond those assembled by the councils of England's King James I in 1608, the Book of Mormon is not just the cornerstone of the LDS religion. It was also anticipated and foreseen by biblical prophecy as necessary in the progression of man's mortal probation. In Ezekiel we read,

> Thou son of man, take thee one stick, and write upon it, for Judah, and for the children of Israel his companions: then take another stick, and write upon it, for Joseph, the stick of Ephraim, and for all the house of Israel his companions: And join them one to another into one stick; and they shall become one in thine hand. . . . And say unto them, Thus saith the Lord God; Behold, I will take the children of Israel from among the heathen, whither they be gone, and will gather them on every side, and bring them into their own land: And I will make them one nation in the land upon the mountains of Israel; and one king shall be king to them all: and they shall be no more two nations, neither shall they be divided into two kingdoms any more at all. (Ezekiel 37:16–17, 21–22)

Now approaching two hundred years, the common belief of the LDS faithful worldwide is that the two "sticks" mentioned in Ezekiel represent the Bible (the stick of Judah) and the Book of Mormon (the stick of Joseph or Ephraim).

Like the Bible is a record of the children of God in the Old World, Latter-day Saints believe the Book of Mormon is a record of God's people who migrated to the American continent. Like the Old Testament, the Book of Mormon is a volume of history that chronicles the development, rise, and fall of early civilizations. Ancient prophets foresaw it as a volume of work that must come to pass. Isaiah wrote,

> For the Lord hath poured out upon you the spirit of deep sleep, and hath closed your eyes: the prophets and your rulers, the seers hath he covered. And the vision of all is become unto you as the words of a book that is sealed, which men deliver to one that is learned, saying, Read this, I pray thee: and he saith, I cannot; for it is sealed: And the book is delivered to him that is not learned, saying, Read this, I pray thee: and he saith, I am not learned. . . . Therefore, behold, I will proceed to do a marvelous work among this people, even a marvelous work and a wonder: for the wisdom of their wise men shall perish, and the understanding of their prudent men shall be hid. (Isaiah 29:10–12, 14)

Perhaps one of the most controversial topics relating to the idea of a Christian faith actually receiving revelation came in 1827 when the young Joseph Smith ("him that is not learned") claimed he had been shown a set of plates containing the record of an ancient people. This record, according to Mormon theology, is the "book that is sealed" mentioned by Isaiah. The book was partially sealed when Joseph Smith recovered it from under a rock on a hillside in upstate New York.

Prior to ascending into heaven, Jesus mentioned to his Apostles those "other sheep" referred to earlier in this chapter. The Book of Mormon tells of Christ's visit to the Americas after his Crucifixion and Resurrection. Mormons believe that this additional tome of scripture fulfills Ezekiel's reference of reuniting the two "sticks" into one common volume. This was further echoed by the Apostle Peter when he wrote, "For the prophecy came not in old time by the will of man: but holy men of God spake as they were moved by the Holy Ghost" (2 Peter 1:21).

Understanding Isaiah's prophecies, which appear in the Old Testament as well as in the Book of Mormon, provides further insight into the fulfillment of the gospel of Christ, his Second Coming, and the general state of mankind prior to the End of Days.

NOTES

1. Contradictions in the Bible, "The Priestly writer's reworking of the Yahwist material of Genesis 1–11," http://contradictionsinthebible.com/the-priestly-writers-reworking-of-the-yahwist-material-of-genesis-1-11/. Accessed April 24, 2018.
2. Dr. K. Wheeler, "What Are the J, E, and P Texts of Genesis?" https://web.cn.edu/kwheeler/Genesis_texts.html. Accessed April 24, 2018.
3. *Christianity Today*, "John Calvin: Father of the Reformed Faith," http://www.christianity-today.com/history/people/theologians/john-calvin.html. Accessed April 24, 2018.
4. A to Z Quotes, http://www.azquotes.com/quote/863803. Accessed April 24, 2018.
5. Bible.org, "The Bible: The Written Word of God," https://bible.org/seriespage/4-bible-written-word-god. Accessed April 24, 2018.
6. Got Questions, "Who are the 'other sheep' mentioned in John 10:16?" https://www.gotquestions.org/other-sheep.html. Accessed April 24, 2018.
7. The Church of Jesus Christ of Latter-day Saints, Newsroom, "Book of Mormon: Another Testament of Jesus Christ," https://www.mormonnewsroom.org/article/book-of-mormon. Accessed April 24, 2018.
8. Canon of the Bible, "The council of Jamnia: AD 90," http://www.bible.ca/b-canon-council-of-jamnia.htm. Accessed April 24, 2018.

CHAPTER 10

RESTORATION OF THE PRE-NICAEAN GOSPEL

From thence he shall come to judge.

—Nicene Creed

A funny thing happened on the way to the Forum.

Actually, it was on the way to what is now Turkey.

Controversy surrounding the divergence between who God is and how he is depicted in the form of a "Holy Trinity" or "Godhead" gave rise during the first and second centuries. While Rome wrestled with the growing masses of Christian converts, who continued to influence the way the empire worshipped its deity, free-thinkers were already shaping the ranks of believers on everything from which direction to point during prayers[1] to who was actually in charge in heaven.

Perhaps the notion of a divine threesome is partially due to the interpretations of the second-century Christian scholar Origen of Alexandria who posited,

> The God and Father, who holds the universe together, is superior to every being that exists, for he imparts to each one from his own existence that which each one is; the Son, being less than the Father, is superior to rational creatures alone (for he is second to the Father); the Holy Spirit is still less, and dwells within the saints alone. So that in this way the power of the Father is greater than that of the Son and of the Holy Spirit, and that of the Son is more than that of the Holy Spirit.[2]

Origen, the son of a martyred Christian philosopher, spent more than twenty years researching and writing about the books of the ancient scriptures, which (at the time) only consisted of the Old Testament.

Origen evaluated the ancient writings based on three principles: literal writings, allegorical accounts, and moral messages. As no consensus of doctrine existed among the disparate congregations throughout the empire, Origen's early "De Principiis"[3] is often referred to as the foundation on which Christian philosophy is synthesized and blended into and with Greek and Roman ideologies. Origen's views on the Holy Trinity were based on a hierarchical model, with one divine being, "God in the fullest," sitting above all others; the Son, "Logos Dunamis"; and the accompanying Holy Spirit, being elected powers.[4]

Arius, another Christian leader from Alexandria during the latter half of the fourth century, argued that Christ was a divine being created by God (because of the consistent scriptural reference to him as the "Son of God") prior to the formation of the world. Based on a sort of "Celestial Hierarchy" called "Neoplatonism,"[5] this concept of a sort-of divine trifecta has its origins loosely rooted in the writings of Justin Martyr, who was an early Christian apologist who died in AD 165. Justin, who was executed in Rome for not worshiping the gods, wrote, "No one with even the slightest intelligence would dare to assert that the Creator of all things left his super-celestial realms to make himself visible in a little spot on earth."[6]

Subsequently, any theological reference to a divine interaction between God and man, including the creation of the world, would not be undertaken (as Justin supposed) by an almighty deity but would have been undertaken by one who was assigned the responsibility and considered as the "Logos," or "Lord," or (as implied in earlier writings by Plato) the pre-mortal Jesus.

By contrast, Alexander, who was the current bishop of Rome,[7] disagreed, arguing that Arius's position implied that Jesus was less than God the Father, which suggested some form of divine hierarchy (and further insinuated that any Holy Roman Emperor may not be capable of divine rule).

Alexander believed that Christ and God were of the same "essence," and soon the controversy over the nature of God and his relationship to Jesus became central to religious debate throughout the empire. Add to the mix another perspective, one suggested by third-century priest and theologian Sabellius. In Sabellius's view, God was a single, indivisible entity comprised of the Father, Son, and Holy Ghost.

This form of "monarchian modalism"[8] suggested a divine being or god who could live, die, regenerate, and sanctify his comings and goings at will. And while seemingly outlandish by some standards (and a view that got Sabellius kicked out of the Catholic Church by Pope Callistus in 220), with some sense of irony, various church scholars would suggest that in one interpretation or another, it is this divine modalism[9] that currently abounds as the core belief around God for today's current Christian population.

Such views, however, suggested a flaw in the rule of governance for ancient Rome and would not stand with the political factions (or the emperor).

At the beginning of the fourth century AD, Rome was replete with people claiming to have a portion of the original Church of Christ. There were many other interpretations of who and what Jesus was. In one case, a bishop from northern Africa actually believed that Jesus was sent to rescue mankind from a blind, crazed fallen angel who had made the earth without authorization.

After his conquest and reunification of the Roman Empire, Constantine turned his focus on matters concerning these disparate ideologies and deciding on what date the empire should celebrate Easter.

In the summer of 325, the emperor decided that at the expense of the government and under his personal supervision, all of the leaders of the various Christian sects would be gathered in Nicaea. Their purpose was to define, once and for all, the nature of Jesus and his role in deity. This council, he supposed (and declared), would quell the rising disputations among the faithful regarding a notion that Christ was not divine but created in the flesh. Under the so-called "objective" guidance of Constantine himself, a vote was taken, and Arius's views were designated as heretical.

One fast track to breeding controversy is to second-guess the status quo, and that's what was happening in fourth-century Rome. Arius was not just out-voted at the council. He was also thrown out of the church.

Out of that council of deep thinkers, philosophers, political figures, and pontificators came the Nicene Creed. The Creed, which established the foundation for Christian ideology, was an attempt to unify three centuries of interpretation about the nature of Jesus and his relationship to God. It would define what has come to be referred to by the general Christian world as the "Holy Trinity" and establish more than fifteen hundred years of the fundamental Christian view on the nature of God and his relationship with Jesus.

Let's look at what the Creed actually says:

We believe in one God, the Father Almighty, Maker of all things visible and invisible.

And in one Lord Jesus Christ, the Son of God, begotten of the Father [the only-begotten; that is, of the essence of the Father, God of God,] Light of Light, very God of very God, begotten, not made, being of one substance with the Father;

By whom all things were made;

Who for us men, and for our salvation, came down and was incarnate and was made man;

He suffered, and the third day he rose again, ascended into heaven;

From thence he shall come to judge the quick and the dead. And in the Holy Ghost.[10]

Even though early Christian leaders conjectured on the nature and composition of the Holy Trinity, until Nicaea, no one proclaimed the doctrine of the Trinity as currently accepted.

Almost sixty years after the Council at Nicaea, church leaders felt the need to revise the language further while also financing the illumination and publishing of fifty volumes of authorized scripture that would contain the first version of the "New Testament." These volumes were distributed to congregational leadership of "authorized" parishioners with its content spread throughout the Holy Roman Empire. It provided the only allowed religious canon of the day, while also fostering conjecture over what God's word *really* meant to the common folk and what God expected from his faithful followers.

Move the calendar forward about sixteen hundred years to 1820s New England, and Christian thought further fractures with the notion that a restoration of the pre-Nicene church structure has been restored in the form of a "latter-day restoration." Given the early ideas devised by Origen, Arias, and their peers, the eschatology of man might yet have another piece of the puzzle as more Christians agree with the ancient Apostle John in that they, like the Lord himself, "can do nothing . . . but what [they] seeth the Father do" (John 5:19).

The Bible states that God made each of us in his own image. With the advent of Mormonism and the revelations by Joseph Smith in the mid-nineteenth century, the LDS faithful believe God is a glorified being who has attained eternal perfection in all things. Though the thought of being compared to God would send many Christians into a stupor of fear and confusion (probably much like those fourth-century Christian scholars), Latter-day Saints believe that the ultimate gift God can bestow on his children is to give them all that he has. This, in turn, glorifies him even more, just as earthly parents are edified by the growth, development, and success of their children.

In a sense of modern alignment with the theologies of Origen and Arias, the LDS belief system includes the idea that God is literally the spirit father of all mankind[11] (including Jesus Christ), which is also referenced by many ancient prophets:

And lo a voice from heaven, saying, this is my beloved Son, in whom I am well pleased. (Matthew 3:17)

There came a voice out of the cloud, saying, this is my beloved Son: hear him. (Luke 9:35)

The Son can do nothing of himself, but what he seeth the Father do. (John 5:19)

Whether out of curiosity or rooted in a deeper sense of divine purpose, humans seem to want to learn more about where we came from, why we are here, and where we will go when our respective lives come to a close. It's also been shown throughout history that change can be painful—even disruptive—especially where politics and religion are concerned.

What becomes accepted as a common belief offers a certain level of comfort, which has historically lulled societies to form opinions and belief systems, often around word-of-mouth that has been handed down from one generation to the next. What was once defined as doctrine fades into legend and eventually becomes myth (like the idea that God could possibly be one of three distinct personages, as was accepted by the early faithful). By contrast, we're always discovering something new that, prior to that discovery, might have been considered fiction—or even heresy.

That's human nature.

What's also human nature is the desire to try to interpret and justify political dictates into dogma, such as the notion that the original creed should be interpreted as "God in Three Persons." Nowhere in the Nicene Creed does the discourse suggest

God was three different people, and while modern Christian orthodoxy accepts such interpretations, much of those perspectives are rooted in ancient filibusters by princes, priests, and politicians.

NOTES

1. E-notes, "What is the direction that Christians pray to God?" https://www.enotes.com/homework-help/what-directions-which-christian-pray-god-354692. Accessed April 24, 2018.
2. Eric George Jay, Origen's Treatise on Prayer (Eugene, OR: WIPF & Stock, 1954), 55.
3. Early Church Texts, "Origen the Preface to De Principiis—Latin Text and English translation," http://www.earlychurchtexts.com/public/origen_de_principiis_preface.htm. Accessed April 24, 2018.
4. Stanford Encyclopedia of Philosophy, Mark J. Edwards, "Origen," https://plato.stanford.edu/entries/origen/, April 18, 2018. Accessed April 24, 2018.
5. Stanford Encyclopedia of Philosophy, Dale Tuggy, "History of Trinitarian Doctrines," https://plato.stanford.edu/entries/trinity/trinity-history.html, 2016. Accessed April 24, 2018.
6. StackExchange, Christianity, questions/answers, "Who made the distinction between heaven vs. sky explicitly," https://christianity.stackexchange.com/questions/60670/who-made-the-distinction-between-heaven-vs-sky-explicitly/60689. Accessed April 24, 2018.
7. New World Encyclopedia, "Pope Alexander I," http://www.newworldencyclopedia.org/entry/Pope_Alexander_I. Accessed April 24, 2018.
8. New World Encyclopedia, "Monarchianism," http://www.newworldencyclopedia.org/entry/Monarchianism. Accessed April 24, 2018.
9. Theopedia, "Modalism," https://www.theopedia.com/modalism. Accessed April 24, 2018.
10. To download a free copy of the entire Nicene Creed, see http://www.anglicancommunion.org/media/109020/Nicene-Creed.pdf. Accessed April 24, 2018.
11. LDS.org, "Prophecies in the Bible about Joseph Smith," George A. Horton Jr., https://www.lds.org/ensign/1989/01/prophecies-in-the-bible-about-joseph-smith?lang=eng. (See also Ensign magazine, The Church of Jesus Christ of Latter-day Saints, July 1989.) Accessed April 24, 2018.

CHAPTER 11

CHURCH AND KINGDOM TAKEN FROM THE EARTH

A famine in the land.

—Amos 8:11–12

Does God speak to his children anymore?

If scripture is to be judged on a historical time line, God seemed to remain mum for almost two thousand years, and the direction in which his worshippers were to take was lost to the ages. This became well demonstrated as the various Christian sects began to divide and appear[1] throughout the Roman Empire during the first five centuries after the death of Christ.

As scholars examine the contents and context of the Old and New Testaments, much of what was written about how to behave in accordance with God's will (a.k.a.: "church life") has changed over time through different languages, cultures, and ideologies. In some cases, as in the Psalms and portions of Isaiah, guidelines for how God wanted his followers to act, where he wanted them to go, and what he wanted them to do were clear. In Exodus we read,

> And this day shall be unto you for a memorial; and ye shall keep it a feast to the Lord throughout your generations; ye shall keep it a feast by an ordinance for ever. . . . And in the first day there shall be an holy convocation, and in the seventh day there shall be an holy convocation to you; no manner of work shall be done in them, save that which every man must eat, that only may be done of you. (Exodus 12:14, 16)

The notion that a community within an empire would follow someone other than the emperor did not sit well in the courts of Rome.[2] It was one thing to manage the Jews (who had been complaining about their oppression for generations) and their traditional subculture. But it was another to consider that a wandering man from the deserts of Galilee and a handful of his followers could sway even the Jews to rethink their religious position. Thus, the Christian persecution began. Both Jew and Gentile began to follow the words of Jesus as taught by his appointed Apostles, which resulted in tremendous losses, tragedy, and almost the total extinction of an entire culture.

The ancient Church of Christ was established based on a hierarchal structure[3] with various roles, including evangelists, ministers, and other religious leaders who were called into specific positions for the administration of the Church. The organization and structure of the Church continued under the anointing of Peter, who was given the keys of authority by Jesus prior to his Ascension. Peter held those keys until his death in Rome in AD 66. Subsequent Apostles, including Andronicus, Steven, Barnabas, and even the great Apostle Paul, served as special witnesses of Christ's teaching under the direction of Peter.

James, the brother of Christ, for example, although not one of the original Twelve Apostles, was called to the apostleship after the Resurrection. He eventually served as a bishop in Jerusalem (chosen and anointed by Peter) according to the first-century writings of Clement of Rome:

> To James, the lord, and the bishop of bishops, who rules Jerusalem, the holy church
> of the Hebrews, and the churches everywhere excellently rounded by the providence
> of God, with the elders and deacons, and the rest of the brethren, peace be always.[4]

By way of odd coincidence, there were at least three major references to different men named James in the New Testament. "James the Just," who was the brother of Jesus,[5] wrote the Epistle of James in the New Testament; James, the son of Zebedee, who was one of the Lord's closest personal assistants (along with John, the other son of Zebedee, and Peter); and James, the son of Alphaeus, who was also one of Jesus's original Twelve.

The Roman leaders always had spies plugged into the most fashionable trendy groups, like those associated with James and his rising tide of followers. Rome's reaction was swift and firm, resulting in a total occupation of Jerusalem and Roman leadership. According to historical accounts, they were quick to silence heretical religious factions opposed to the state religion. For the Roman leaders, the catch of the day was one of these Apostles, which led to the Sanhedrin ordering Clement's "bishop of bishops" to be thrown from the pinnacle of the temple and clubbed to death.[6] With the exception of John and Judas, all of Jesus's original Apostles met with terrible demise at the hands of their captors.

The following list illustrates the most popular version of the fates of the original Twelve Apostles of Jesus. Each of the original twelve men called by Jesus, with the exception of Judas Iscariot and John the Beloved, was summarily hunted down throughout the empire and either murdered on the spot or made part of a public execution.[7]

APOSTLE	CAUSE OF DEATH	APPROX. YR.
Judas Iscariot	Driven by guilt, committed suicide by hanging	34
Bartholomew	Beaten, crucified, and beheaded	52
Phillip	Crucified at Heirapole Phryga	52
Thomas	Impaled by lance while preaching in the East Indies (some accounts say he was in India)	52
Matthew	Killed by sword in Ethiopia	60
James (son of Alphaeus)	Crucified in Egypt	60
James (brother of John)	Beheaded by command of Herod	64
Simon Peter	Crucified head down on a hill outside Rome	66
Thaddaeus	Shot in Arafat by Roman soldiers	72
Andrew	Bound and crucified in Greece by order of the Governor	74
Simon Zelotes	Crucified in Persia	74
John the Beloved	Banished to the island of Patmos	96

Although there are many recorded interpretations on the actual method of death, what is important is that these men all died for their holy cause, while John the Beloved was banished to the island of Patmos in AD 96.[8]

Like most Christians of antiquity, the Christians throughout the empire did not congregate into single groups but would choose instead to meet in house churches and study the word of the Lord as referenced by Paul in his letter to members of the Church in Rome. Paul writes,

> Greet Priscilla and Aquila my helpers in Christ Jesus . . . unto whom not only I give thanks, but also all the churches of the Gentiles. . . . Likewise greet the church that is in their house. Salute my well-beloved Epænetus, who is the firstfruits of Achaia unto Christ. (Romans 16:3–5)

With the last Apostles rounded up and executed, however, the Church no longer had direct leadership, and a whole new wave of people rose up to become self-appointed leaders. Consequently, religious chapters that were organized by the likes of Steven, James, Timothy, and Paul were left to their own designs and influences of the local cultures.

Under the Roman Caesars, the empire took less than a century to finally destroy God's anointed leaders. By the end of the first century, the holy apostleship, under the divine authority granted to them by Christ, vanished from the earth. Some Christian interpretation of scripture, combined with belief in modern-day revelation, contends that the heavens were closed to mankind, resulting in a separation between God and his children. This is referred to more commonly as the Great Apostasy, which was foreseen by the prophets and recorded in both Old and New Testament accounts. The following is found in Isaiah and Amos in the Old Testament:

> The earth also is defiled under the inhabitants thereof; because they have transgressed the laws, changed the ordinance, broken the everlasting covenant. . . . Therefore hath the curse devoured the earth, and they that dwell therein are desolate: therefore the inhabitants of the earth are burned, and few men left. . . . Behold, the days come, saith the Lord God, that I will send a famine in the land, not a famine of bread, nor a thirst for water, but of hearing the words of the Lord: And they shall wander from sea to sea, and from the north even to the east, they shall run to and fro to seek the word of the Lord, and shall not find it. (Isaiah 24:5–6; Amos 8:11–12)

Subsequently, scores of people, mostly Christian factionalists, were slaughtered at the games in the Flavian Amphitheater, which was more commonly known as the Colosseum. The Colosseum was commissioned by the emperor Vespasian in AD 69 and was later completed by his son Titus. According to historical records, during its first full year of operation, an average of one person was killed every five minutes around the clock as part of the Romans' pagan (and often carnal) festivities. These killings usually took place in mock battles and executions.[9] They spanned nearly four hundred years, with an estimated four hundred thousand people and more than one million animals being slaughtered for entertainment.

Rome went through a difficult time during the early years of the first century and into its sunset years in the fifth century at the hands of the Goths. Its borders covered almost all of the Mediterranean, from the shores of the Caspian Sea in the east, to Brittania in the northwest, and Egypt in the south. Maintaining not only an empire but also such a vast cross-cultural community grew more challenging for the Senate and Caesar, and the last thing on their minds was the idea that a new faith would rise up and topple the old gods.

By the beginning of the fourth century, Rome was so large it was the edict of the emperor Diocletian that four lesser kings (two Augustuses and two Caesars) assisted in leadership to fend off the barbarian enemies from the north (the Goths, Vandals, and the like). The tetrarchy, as it was known,[10] was not successful, and within a few years, everybody wanted the throne for themselves.

One of the four leaders, Constantine,[11] was the son of a Roman senator and a

Christian-convert wife. Constantine became a powerful military leader and eventually rose to become the Western Caesar. By the fourth century, the whispers of the Good Shepherd and his Apostles had grown into a shout across the empire. Adding ambivalence to insult, Christian factions were rising in numbers. This new religion threatened to kick even Jupiter himself—the supreme deity of the ancient Romans—off his throne. It shook the Roman Empire to its core in AD 313, when Constantine defined imperial edict that protected the rights of the growing population of Christian worship throughout the empire.

A consistent precept associated with mankind's relationship with the one true God has to do with the concept that he talks to his children, gives them instructions, and commands them in the way they should live and worship. As Paul wrote to Timothy,

> All scripture is given by inspiration of God, and is profitable for doctrine, for reproof, for correction, for instruction in righteousness: That the man of God may be perfect, throughly furnished unto all good works. (2 Timothy 3:16–17)

Not many people outside the high priests of the ancient temple were allowed to see, handle, read, or even possess holy works. Whether out of affordability or by divine commandment (interpreted or otherwise), this limited access to scripture also meant the government of God fell upon the learned few who were fortunate enough—or otherwise—to possess the ability to interpret God's commandments based on a variety of motivations. By the time of the final demise of Christ's Apostles, misinterpretations throughout the Roman Empire (and God's children—both Jew and Gentile convert) began to surface, spread, and abound.

The Roman Empire was not completely without civility, however. The three major cities of Rome, Alexandria (in Egypt), and Antioch (in Syria) were social hot spots[12] during the early centuries of the first millennium. They were also large centers of Jewish culture, which had become highly influential in maintaining self-governing control over their territory. They became melting pots for independent thinkers, sophists, and further pontification over the word of God.

Greek philosophies and other local customs became stronger influences among the Christian factions. By the close of the second century, there were house churches and Christian spin-offs covering almost every major region of the empire. Some efforts were made to keep the foundation of the Church intact, the most notable being that of Ignatius of Antioch in about AD 108, but even his efforts were made while he was on his way to his own execution in Rome.

The Church of God, as it was organized by Christ and further established by the Apostles throughout the lands, was gone from its original state, and so was its authority. Over the course of the next several centuries, religious factionalism began to creep into the Roman government, and secularism infiltrated the pure Church of God. By AD 476, when the Goths, a heathen tribe from the north, overran Rome, any remote traces of the original church were gone from the world.

NOTES

1. *Christianity Today*, Christian History, Charles E. Hummel, "The church at home: the house church movement," http://www.christianitytoday.com/history/issues/issue-9/church-at-home-house-church-movement.html. Accessed April 25, 2018.

2. *Christianity Today*, Christian History, Everett Ferguson, "Persecution in the Early Church: Did You Know?" http://www.christianitytoday.com/history/issues/issue-27/persecution-in-early-church-did-you-know.html. Accessed April 25, 2018.

3. Facts and Details, Jeffrey Hays, "Early Christian Churches and Church Structure," http://factsanddetails.com/world/cat55/sub353/item1405.html, 2011. Accessed April 25, 2018.

4. Epistle of Clement, Bible Study Tools, "Epistle of Clement to James," https://www.biblestudytools.com/history/early-church-fathers/ante-nicene/vol-8-third-fourth-centuries/pseudo-clementine-literature/epistle-of-clement-to-james.html. Accessed April 24, 2018.

5. Early Church History 101, "James, the Brother of Jesus," http://www.churchhistory101.com/century1-p6.php. Accessed April 25, 2018.

6. Christian History for Every Man, Paul F. Pavao, "The Death of James the Just, Brother of Jesus," https://www.christian-history.org/death-of-james.html, 2009. Accessed April 25, 2018.

7. StackExchange, Christianity, "How did the apostles die?" https://christianity.stackexchange.com/questions/23853/how-did-the-apostles-die. Accessed April 25, 2018.

8. Answers from the Book, "Was the Apostle John Exiled to the Isle of Patmos?" http://answersfromthebook.net/was-the-apostle-john-exiled-to-the-isle-of-patmos-if-so-who-exiled-him-and-why/. Accessed April 25, 2018.

9. The Colossevm [Colosseum], Maurice M. Hasset, "The Coliseum and the Martyrs," transcribed by Joseph P. Thomas, http://www.the-colosseum.net/history/martyrium_en.htm. Accessed April 25, 2018.

10. Lumen Learning, Boundless World History, "The Diocletian and the Tetrarchy," https://courses.lumenlearning.com/suny-hccc-worldhistory/chapter/diocletian-and-the-tetrarchy/. Accessed April 25, 2018.

11. *Christianity Today*, Christian History, "Constantine," http://www.christianitytoday.com/history/people/rulers/constantine.html. Accessed on April 25, 2018.

12. Ancient History Encyclopedia, Joshua J. Mark, "Alexandria, Egypt," https://www.ancient.eu/alexandria/, April 28, 2011. Accessed April 25, 2018.

CHAPTER 12

CHRISTIANITY AND
TRUTH RESTORED

The power of an endless life.

—Hebrews 7:16

The Roman Empire wasn't the best place to practice Christianity during the first and second centuries. The disciples of Jesus went underground and formed house churches after the mass slaughter of the general Christian population by Nero during the mid-70s. Competing philosophies emerged almost immediately. New Testament accounts between Peter and Paul, for example, reveal differences in opinion about various doctrines, as well as how to govern the faithful followers of Christ, but both agree in the general form of who stood at the head of the faith: the Lord himself. In Ephesians 2 we read,

> Now therefore ye are no more strangers and foreigners, but fellow citizens with the saints, and of the household of God; And are built upon the foundation of the apostles and prophets, Jesus Christ himself being the chief corner stone. (Ephesians 2:19–20)

The Holy Bible not only provides an early record of the children of God; it also foreshadows and testifies of the life and times of Jesus Christ. The Bible has influenced the Christian world for hundreds of generations. Its many historical accounts span from the beginning of man through the life of Christ and into our future. Buried in the many biblical iterations and interpretations are found important aspects that serve as spiritual pointers to what some Christian sects believe to be indications of a spiritual drought caused by the absence of God's kingdom on earth, but with the promise of its restoration.

The Old Testament includes the body of religious work used by the Jews of ancient times, which was also later accepted by the followers of Christ. Much like the ancient Church, the actual contents of the Bible, however, have varied through the ages.[1] Many interpretations have been made, negotiated, and even fought over. Books contained in the Old Testament were written over centuries of time and assembled from a body of work spanning hundreds of miles by many authors.

By contrast, the contents of the New Testament came from a few sources and were written during a short period of time, probably within the first one hundred years following the life of Jesus while the ancient Church was still under the direction of his Apostles.

The Old Testament provides the earliest accepted history of God's kingdom on earth. Moses was God's chosen leader around 1500 BC and was noted as the principal leader of God's kingdom in the earliest years of his Church on the earth. The Old Testament is a collection of books that were written prior to the birth of Jesus by people who were designated as God's mouthpieces throughout the earliest years of civilized man. These books include testimonials, songs, poems, prophecies, and words of instruction. The Old Testament also comprises core doctrine for the original Church of God. Modern Christians consider the Old Testament a critical collection of early views into Church government and prophesies of the coming of the Messiah.

The Old Testament denotes the ancient covenant of Moses, the laws given by God for the children of Israel. These laws are often considered as the lesser laws,[2] because Israel was not spiritually prepared for God's higher laws, which came through his higher "Priesthood after the order of Melchizedek." The New Testament provides an account of the Christian ministries of those who were directly involved in the life and ministry of Jesus and who were charged to sustain his Church on the earth.

Traditional Christian theology holds that the sacred passages within the Old and New Testaments are literal translations out of the mouth of God himself. Historical discoveries, hundreds of years of additional manuscripts, research, and further scholarship, however, contend that many of the verses, although inspired and directed by God, in many aspects fall short of being a complete body of divine revelation, because the formal doctrine of Christ was lost in the Great Apostasy at the close of the first century.

Our ability to progress to greater levels of knowledge and understanding is enhanced by our willingness to accept the possibility that we don't know everything and that the will of the Lord, while offered only in glimpses, needed to be removed and restored to the earth, as was prophesied by the likes of Isaiah, Amos, Matthew, and Jesus himself. The following admonitions are recorded in Matthew:

> Watch and pray, lest you enter into temptation. The spirit indeed is willing but the flesh is weak. . . . Take heed that no man deceive you. For many shall come in my name, saying, I am Christ; and shall deceive many. . . . For nation shall rise against nation, and kingdom against kingdom: and there shall be famines, and pestilences, and earthquakes, in divers places. . . . And many false prophets shall rise, and shall deceive many. (Matthew 26:41; 24:4–5, 7, 11)

The law of Moses, which preceded the fulfillment of the life of Christ, was to be strictly adhered to as the principal foundation of God's Church on the earth and included the law of "carnal commandments"[3] (worldly commandments that include directions essential to living by the edicts of the day). From a symbolic perspective, these carnal laws could be mapped to the fundamental principles of the gospel of Jesus, which are faith, repentance, baptism by immersion, and receiving the Holy Ghost by one who is authorized to perform this ordinance by holding a specific kind of priesthood. In Hebrews we read,

> For it is evident that our Lord sprang out of Judah; of which tribe Moses spake nothing concerning priesthood. And it is yet far more evident: for that after the similitude of Melchisedec there ariseth another priest, who is made, not after the law of a carnal commandment, but after the power of an endless life. (Hebrews 7:14–16)

God tipped off Moses while the two of them were spending quality time in the mountains above Pharaoh's empire. He informed him that in direct disobedience to his order to behave, the children of Israel had turned their desert settlement into a den of iniquity. When Moses returned from Mount Sinai, having the tablets with the word of God inscribed on them, he threw them down, breaking them at the base of a golden calf.

Contrary to what Mr. DeMille portrayed in his epic film *The Ten Commandments*, there is no scriptural account of the earth opening up and swallowing Edward G. Robinson or anyone else. In fact, a modern-day version of the film would more likely follow the account in Exodus. Moses, after looking out at the naked campers, would instruct the sons of Levi to use their swords and kill all of the infidels (about three thousand of them) in the encampment, because that was the commandment given to him by God regarding the disobedience of those within his Church.

The relevance of these incidents, the contents, as well as the context of the Old and New Testaments, has been lost through misinterpretation and time. In some cases, as in the Psalms and portions of Isaiah, the works were written in a way to be memorized through oral tradition, which further confounded the masses.

Up until the ministry of Jesus, the known population of God's children held to the first five books of the Old Testament as the single volume of divine revelation.

Then Jesus showed up in Jerusalem, and the entire God-fearing world was turned upside down. With the onset of Jesus's ministry and the subsequent witnesses and admonitions by his Apostles, the children of God found new words of inspiration, even a new set of commandments. Such words, which Jesus left behind upon his Ascension into heaven, were always revealed under the direction of one of the Lord's authorized witnesses and inspired by the Holy Ghost.

According to the accounts in the New Testament, the original Twelve Apostles were often instructed by Jesus to minister to both Jew and Gentile and to establish his Church and its directives throughout all peoples and cultures. The Twelve Apostles continued their ministry[4] until all of them were ultimately killed or banished, as mentioned previously.

By the beginning of the fourth century, the conquests of Constantine, who was also the first Roman emperor to convert to Christianity,[5] resulted in reunifying Rome under one leader. Perhaps out of hubris or in some twist of divine inspiration, the Roman regent decided to move the ancient capital of the empire from Rome to the ancient port town of Byzantium on the Black Sea. Historically recognized as the crossroads between Eastern Europe and everything else, moving the capital city to the newly named Constantinople planted the seeds of the destruction of the secular empire of the day, to be replaced by what became a religious empire throughout the world by the close of the first millennium.

Constantine's changing the central capital of the empire from Rome to what is now Istanbul had a significant impact on the religion of the day. It created a religious center in the eastern portion of the region, which was highly influenced by Greek tradition, while the city of Rome was left to the devices of local Christian leaders, who claimed to be the official headquarters of the legacy Church of Christ.

Looking ahead six hundred years to 1074, long after the battle between Leo and John[6] (the respective bishops of Rome and Constantinople in 588), the Roman Catholic Church was fully established as the religious backbone throughout Europe and the known world. In an ironic twist of direction, religious domination was again in full swing in Eastern Europe and the Middle East, but this time without any formal spiritual leadership sanctioned by God. Under the direction of Pope Gregory and the Roman Catholic Church, the first Crusades began, with a focus on ridding the Holy Land of the many religious "infidels" who inhabited it—namely, those who were not Christian (or Catholic).

By the beginning of the seventeenth century, the Roman Catholic Church was the governing body over virtually all of the Christian world.[7] The Vatican's position, strengthened through the Crusades, would ensure a strong religious hold on political and religious heads of state throughout Europe.

But a new era of enlightenment, which focused on secular independence and religious interpretation on the freedoms of worship, began to spread, largely because of Martin Luther's disenchantment with his Catholic leaders.

By the mid-1700s, a third generation of religious persecution was underway as American colonists began to embrace new philosophies on prayer, baptism, and the role of religion in day-to-day life. The Church of England (having itself being formed after splitting from Catholicism) was not pleased with the influx of new religious ideas spawning in America, thanks mostly to the efforts of evangelists such as Jonathan Edwards and George Whitfield.

But the damage was done, and with the "Great Awakening," as was mentioned in an earlier chapter, which was spreading throughout New England in the nineteenth century, the stage was set for the coming forth of a new religion that did not descend from any of the existing Christian sects: Mormonism.[8]

Since God's true and ordained Church vanished from the world, posits the LDS faithful, it would take the right combination of religious, political, and cultural conditions to allow the original Church to be reestablished. There arose no better place than in the colonial states of early America, or a better time than in the early stages of a new nation free from religious and political tyranny.

The LDS philosophy holds that because it was a chosen land, it was in the United States that God chose to restore his kingdom on the earth. It was there that he could reestablish a fullness of his gospel without it suffering another extinction.

As in the organized Church during the time of Jesus, the restoration of fundamental Church precepts would be comprised of a leadership of Twelve Apostles who are called and ordained to the office by one who has received keys directly from the Savior himself. The LDS faith sustains such a man as prophet, seer, and revelator. This new religion believes en masse that he and the others within the Quorum of the Twelve Apostles were called, set apart, and ordained by direction of Jesus through an unbroken line of authority. This line of authority was restored to the Earth through the nineteenth-century LDS Church leader and Prophet Joseph Smith, which laid the groundwork to restore sacred truths and reestablish the Lord's Church in an inspired nation—America.

NOTES

1. Greatsite.com, "English Bible History," http://www.greatsite.com/timeline-english-bible-history/, 1997. Accessed April 25, 2018.
2. *Old Testament Student Manual, Genesis—2 Samuel*, "Exodus 21–24; 31–35, The Mosaic Law: A Preparatory Gospel" (Salt Lake City: The Church of Jesus Christ of Latter-day Saints, 1980), 136–44. See https://www.lds.org/manual/old-testament-student-manual-genesis-2-samuel/exodus-21-24-31-35-the-mosaic-law-a-preparatory-gospel?lang=eng. Accessed April 25, 2018.
3. BYU Religious Studies Center, Edward J. Brandt, "The Law of Moses and the Law of Christ," https://rsc.byu.edu/archived/sperry-symposium-classics-old-testament/law-moses-and-law-christ, 2005. Accessed April 25, 2018.
4. Agape Bible Study, Michal Hunt, "Why Did the Apostles and Disciples Stay in Jerusalem after the Crucifixion of Jesus of Nazareth?" http://www.agapebiblestudy.com/documents/Why%20the%20Apostles%20and%20Disciples%20Stayed%20in%20Jerusalem.htm, 2008. Accessed April 25, 2018.
5. The Web Chronology Project, Corrie Ferguson and Amy M. Grupp, "Constantine Converts to Christianity," ed. Jamie Griesmer and Peter B. VerHage, res. Emily McCarty and Elizabeth M. Mosbo, http://www.thenagain.info/WebChron/EastEurope/ConstantineConverts.html, 1996. Accessed April 25, 2018.
6. Revolvy.com, "Siege of Dorostolon," https://www.revolvy.com/main/index.php?s=Siege%20of%20Dorostolon&item_type=topic. Accessed April 25, 2018.
7. MuséeProtestant.org, "The Catholic reforming movements in 17th century France," https://www.museeprotestant.org/en/notice/the-catholic-reforming-movements-in-seventeenth-century-france/. Accessed April 25, 2018.
8. Mormon Newsroom, "Mormonism 101: What Is Mormonism?" https://www.mormonnewsroom.org/article/mormonism-101. Accessed April 25, 2018.

Part III

Advancements and Regressions

Anima nostra immortalis et non moriatur.

Our soul is immortal and never dies.[1] (Plato)

The long, dark journey . . .

Part three provides sixteen individual snapshots of the history and social evolution of Christian religions throughout the post-apostolic period. By no means is this designed to be a definitive treatise on Christianity, but any study on the signs leading up to the last dispensation must consider the time line and intersections between Jews and Gentiles, as was foreseen by the ancient prophets, and how those events unfolded down through the ages.

Early writings found in the Old and New Testaments suggest that the intersection between God's favoring the Jews and his turning to the Gentile nations for their redemption set in motion a series of global evolutionary events that have continued to serve as unifier as well as disrupter for cultures and faiths all around the world for two thousand years.

During his mortal ministry, Jesus warned his disciples to be cautious of those who would try to sway them into thinking that he was directing them, or that they were Jesus himself who had returned as foretold by the ancient prophets. In Matthew, the writer records Jesus as saying that many will come to deceive, and they "shall hear of wars and rumors of wars."[2] Christian tradition refers to the "Great Tribulation"[3] as a time mentioned by Jesus as being a period of perpetual unrest in society, families, and the hearts of men.

By the middle of the fourteenth century, as the Dark Ages reached their dimmest period, the world was losing between one third and one half of the entire human race to the Black Death. This was the second pandemic that impacted Europe, with the great plague of 541 being the first, often referred to as the "Plague of Justinian,"[4] which claimed 45 percent of the entire Roman Empire from Egypt to Constantinople.

Despite the mortal frailties, mankind progressed through the pestilence to see advancements in science, technology, and medicine. Each of these developments posed a challenge in one form or another in the conflict between the spiritual welfare and social evolution of mankind,[5] and the status quo of religious thought was right in the middle of the tumult. While wickedness and carnal chaos are often balanced in religious discourse with overcoming economic struggle and persecution, one surefire indication of this being the last dispensation is to check those ancient signs against the moral condition of the civilizations of today's world.

As if the world isn't already in enough turmoil, modern revelation teaches that Christ will return during a time of worldwide strife, corruption, and evil more widespread than has yet to be seen.

Notes

1. See Goodreads.com, https://www.goodreads.com/quotes/568601-have-you-ever-sensed-that-our-soul-is-immortal-and. Accessed May 11, 2018.
2. See Matthew 24:6, the Authorized King James Version of the Holy Bible.
3. Jehovah's Witnesses, "What Is the Great Tribulation?" https://www.jw.org/en/bible-teachings/questions/great-tribulation/. Accessed May 2, 2018.
4. FluTrackers.com, Wikipedia, "Plague of Justinian," https://flutrackers.com/forum/forum/welcome-to-the-scientific-library/pandemics-in-literature/20617-the-plague-of-justinian-ad-541-542. Accessed May 2, 2018.
5. Brought to Life Science Museum, "Belief and Medicine," http://broughttolife.sciencemuseum.org.uk/broughttolife/themes/belief. Accessed May 2, 2018.

CHAPTER 13

THE TIMES OF THE GENTILES COME TO PASS

The kingdom of God is nigh at hand.

—Luke 21:31

Who are the Gentiles, and why do they get their own "appointed times?"

After deliberating on the impending destruction of Jerusalem, Jesus referred to a time when the Gentile nations would reign "until the appointed time of nations" (see Luke 21:24).

In Luke's account of the Savior's teachings, he refers to a period when "the times of the Gentiles are fulfilled." Although there are numerous perspectives on what and when the "times of the Gentiles"[1] may be or have been, the virtual annihilation of the Christian population by Nero in AD 70 certainly points to a time when Gentiles were running amok. And what of Jerusalem being surrounded by armies?

Does the overthrow of the ancient city and the toppling of the temple site indicate the fulfillment of the prophecy regarding the time of the Gentiles?

In his subsequent parable to describe the End of Days, the Savior focused his analogy on the fig tree:

Behold the fig tree, and all the trees; When they now shoot forth, ye see and know of your own selves that summer is now nigh at hand. So likewise ye, when ye see these things come to pass, know ye that the kingdom of God is nigh at hand. Verily I say unto you, this generation shall not pass away, till all be fulfilled. Heaven and earth shall pass away: but my words shall not pass away. (Luke 21:29–33)

Jesus pointed to the fig tree and used it as a symbol of the closing "season" for his people to prepare for his return and redemption of a fallen world and lost flock. The key might be found in an ancient Greek word from the original writing of the Gospel of Luke. The word *kai·ros* is used to mean an appointed measure of time.[2]

In Greek, and in reference to Luke, kai·ros also applies to future events and times. It refers to God's time line and how events apply to the passing of prophecy and the fulfillment of Christ's role as Redeemer of the world as referenced by Paul in his first letter to Thessalonica. He writes,

> But of the times and the seasons, brethren, ye have no need that I write unto you. For yourselves know perfectly that the day of the Lord so cometh as a thief in the night. (1 Thessalonians 5:1–2)

In his letter, Paul refers to a "season" (or *kai-ron* in Greek) in which there is no need to refer to what is inevitable. Following the destruction of Jerusalem by King Nebuchadnezzar II of Babylon in 597 BC, the people of Judah were taken into captivity, and the royal bloodline of King David through Jehoiakim ended. Prophets from both regions (Israel to the north and Judah to the south) foresaw the coming of a time when Gentiles would dominate the age of man, but in the last days, following great success, strife, conquest, and calamity, a son of David (Jesus) would return, reclaim his children, and rule his kingdom. Zechariah prophesied the following:

> I will gather all nations against Jerusalem to battle; and the city shall be taken, and the houses rifled, and the women ravished; and half of the city shall go forth into captivity, and the residue of the people shall not be cut off from the city. Then shall the Lord go forth, and fight against those nations, as when he fought in the day of battle. And his feet shall stand in that day upon the mount of Olives, which is before Jerusalem on the east, and the mount of Olives shall cleave in the midst thereof toward the east and toward the west, and there shall be a very great valley; and half of the mountain shall remove toward the north, and half of it toward the south. (Zechariah 14:2–4)

Modern interpretation of biblical references to the times of the Gentiles suggest that this is a reference to the Lord exacting his retribution on the world, as further referenced by traditional Old Testament and Talmudic philosophy. In the traditional Hebrew writings found throughout the Old Testament, "Those who are in Judea flee[ing] to the mountains" refers not to the retribution of any particular nation or people, but more likely refers to God's Final Judgment against those who stood against him.

Christian scholars usually agree that Christ will establish his kingdom in the geographical region known as Jerusalem, and those who are descendants of Israel will be sustained as part of his sanctuary as was foreseen in Ezekiel. Ezekiel writes,

> I will make a covenant of peace with them; it shall be an everlasting covenant with them: and I will place them, and multiply them, and will set my sanctuary in the midst of them for evermore. My tabernacle also shall be with them: yea, I will be their God, and they shall be my people. (Ezekiel 37:26)

Others are not sure if "the nation of Israel" is referring to a literal place or to a people.[3] In his letter to the faithful of Rome, found in Ephesians, Paul states that we are adopted into God's family through the Atonement and Resurrection. This further suggests that the time of the Gentiles might imply a time of redemption for everyone who is righteous. He declares,

> Ye have received the Spirit of adoption, whereby we cry, Abba, Father. . . . Having predestinated us unto the adoption of children by Jesus Christ to himself, according to the good pleasure of his will, to the praise of the glory of his grace, wherein he hath made us accepted in the beloved. . . . That in the dispensation of the fulness of times he might gather together in one all things in Christ, both which are in heaven, and which are on earth; even in him. (Romans 8:15; Ephesians 1:5–6, 10)

Scholars and historians have debated the nature of the parable of the fig tree, as well as what exactly the "times of the Gentiles" refers to. Most agree that the period of uprising against the children of Israel has more to do with the rise of nations not associated with Judaism. It refers to those that developed based on the other popular faiths, such as Christianity, Islam, Hinduism, and Buddhism. By contrast, since the first century, the social evolution of these four subsequent religions has led to the social, economic, and academic advancement of most of the known world, as noted by the following 2018 statistics:[4]

Christianity[5]	2.4 billion	48 state or preferred religions
Islam[6]	1.8 billion	27 state or preferred religions
Hinduism[7]	1.1 billion	9 state or preferred religions
Buddhism[8]	488 million	7 state or preferred religions

Some Christian scholars point to a time in the future to justify Jesus's remarks as a means of laying the groundwork along a twenty-century-long path for Judaism to recognize its place as needing redemption from the fall of man—just like the Gentile world. Like grafted branches into a fruit tree, the original chosen people of God, many scholars suggest, must be grafted into the kingdom of God by recognizing the Atonement and their redemption by the very man they delivered to the Romans for execution more than two thousand years ago.

So is this the time of the Gentiles and is it coming to a close? Are we living in a time that tries men's souls? While historians and scholars may disagree on the physical location of where exactly the Lord will return and make his final stand against the wickedness of the world, all agree that the time of redemption is near, whether for Jew or Gentile, and God is probably not going to have much patience with anyone who is not on his side.

Notes

1. *Encyclopedia of Mormonism*, "Fullness of Gentiles," http://eom.byu.edu/index.php/Gentiles,_Fulness_of. Accessed May 2, 2018.
2. Bible Study Tools, "Kairos," https://www.biblestudytools.com/lexicons/greek/nas/kairos.html. Accessed May 2, 2018.
3. BYU Religious Studies Center, "Adoption and Atonement: Becoming Sons and Daughters of Christ," https://rsc.byu.edu/archived/volume-6-number-3-2005/adoption-and-atonement-becoming-sons-and-daughters-christ. Accessed May 2, 2018.
4. The Guardian, "More than 20% of countries have official state religions—survey," https://www.theguardian.com/world/2017/oct/03/more-than-20-percent-countries-have-official-state-religions-pew-survey. Accessed May 2, 2018.
5. Wikipedia, "Christianity by Country," https://en.wikipedia.org/wiki/Christianity_by_country. Accessed May 2, 2018.
6. Wikipedia, "History of Islam," https://en.wikipedia.org/wiki/History_of_Islam. Accessed May 2, 2018.
7. Wikipedia, "Hinduism by Country," https://en.wikipedia.org/wiki/Hinduism_by_country. Accessed May 2, 2018.
8. Wikipedia, "Buddhism," https://en.wikipedia.org/wiki/Buddhism. Accessed May 2, 2018.

Chapter 14

Return of the
Ten Tribes

As swift as the eagle flieth.

—Deuteronomy 28:49

Whataloss lost to men may not be lost to God.

That's the general consensus of those who speculate on the conquest, assimilation, and ultimate demise of those classified as the lost ten tribes of Israel.[1]

As accounts from the Old Testament reveal, especially in the books of Leviticus[2] and Deuteronomy,[3] God's covenant people rejected his law and turned away from their obedience. Israel fell into a state of captivity and persecution, the undertones still resonating from the first century to the twenty-first. The greatest consequence for their disobedience, according to scripture, was the scattering of the original nation of Israel among more powerful nations, along with the sacrifice of their lands. More than one ancient prophet warned Israel that,

> I will scatter you among the heathen, and will draw out a sword after you: and your land shall be desolate, and your cities waste. . . . The Lord shall scatter you among the nations, and ye shall be left few in number among the heathen, whither the Lord shall lead you. . . . The Lord shall scatter thee among all people, from the one end of the earth even unto the other; and there thou shalt serve other gods, which neither thou nor thy fathers have known, even wood and stone. . . . I will scatter them also among the heathen, whom neither they nor their fathers have known: and I will send a sword after them, till I have consumed them. (Leviticus 26:33; Deuteronomy 4:27; 28:62, 64; Jeremiah 9:16)

According to ancient Jewish prophecy, one of God's revealed requirements for the world is that the original tribes of Israel will be reunited and all their lands will be restored. The lost tribes of Israel have been debated and pondered for probably as long as they've been . . . well . . . *lost.* Historians and scholars from antiquity, as well as in contemporary times, have evaluated, conjectured, pondered, and pontificated on various verses and parsed passages of scripture in efforts to justify their respective understandings about the fate and anticipated return of these people. But who are these mysterious ten lost tribes,[4] and what happened to them?

Following the covenant God made with the three patriarchs Abraham, Isaac, and Jacob (whose name the Lord changed to "Israel"), Abraham's grandson sired twelve sons, who, in turn, became head of their respective family lines or "tribes." In order of their birth, they are

- Reuben
- Simeon
- Levi
- Judah
- Issachar
- Zebulun
- Dan
- Naphtali
- Gad
- Asher
- Joseph (later replaced by Ephraim and Manasseh)
- Benjamin

Israel's faith in God was predicated upon what God had promised to do for them in the future, while God's covenant with Israel was based upon their obedience. The account documented in the book of Judges is based on the nature and general social decay of a new generation of Israelites who followed the children of Joshua. The new generation of Israel abandoned their religious principles and traded their faith in God for the stone and wooden idols of the surrounding influences, leaving them to face the world without knowing God. In Judges we read the following:

> And also all that generation were gathered unto their fathers: and there rose another generation after them, which knew not the Lord, nor yet the works which he had done for Israel. (Judges 2:10–11)

As described in the Judges, the tribes were united by covenant with God, but eventually shifted their religious and political focus to a more nationalistic form of rule. The charismatic leaders of the time, however (and this is loosely based on scripture that has been interpreted by scholars),[5] the respective hierarchy of leadership within the tribes eventually faded back into tribal or territorial rule in the presence of civil or military unrest. Traditions not sanctioned by the Talmud began to creep into the civic and religious philosophies of Israel as a people, including the worship of idols, which brought upon the children of God his unpleasant wrath and their eviction from their promised lands. Through his prophet, he warns that

> The Lord shall cause thee to be smitten before thine enemies; thou shalt go out one way against them, and flee seven ways before them, and shalt be removed into all the kingdoms of the earth . . . the Lord shall bring a nation against thee from far, from the end of the earth, as swift as the eagle flieth; a nation whose tongue thou shalt not understand. (Deuteronomy 28:25, 49)

Poor Pekah. While the prophets of old—Moses and Isaiah—foresaw a time of wickedness when God's children would fall out of favor, little did Pekah know that the struggle of his kingdom would go on for almost three thousand years. Around 740 BC, under the powerful leadership of Assyrian king Tiglathpeleser III[6] (aka "Pul" in 1 Chronicles), the northern kingdom was conquered and its people taken captive. Shalmaneser[7] and Sargon[8] finished the job twenty years later when they took the northern capital of Samaria. Then, a century later, the southern kingdom of Judah (home of the people known as the Jews) was conquered and dispersed by Nebuchadnezzar II and the nation of Babylon.

After conquering a people, the Assyrians would relocate their captives far away from their native lands, forcing them to blend into Assyrian society and integrate with Assyrian bloodlines and customs. Eventually, the conquered cultures would become so diluted throughout the Assyrian Empire[9] that they would cease to exist as anything but Assyrian.

Although a remnant of Judah remained preserved, many of the Jews began to return to the land of Israel to settle. They remained there until the Romans again destroyed Jerusalem in AD 70, and again in AD 135, which led to Israel again being scattered throughout the many nations of the world. While the descendants of Judah managed to retain remnants of their culture, their history, and their faith, the lost tribes remained scattered throughout the antiquities of time.

While the children of Israel have been restored to a portion of their original land, whose controversial borders are recognized as a sovereign state, the literal gathering of Israel isn't just about reuniting the lost tribes or peacefully restoring them to their former prominence and territories.

Christian historians believe that one key prophecy—one that applies more to our future than our past—is an important sign of the return of the Savior. It is the prophecy that the ten lost tribes of Israel will again be reunited with their cousins from the tribes of Judah, Manasseh, and Ephraim.

Israel's many family branches may be obscure in the eyes of man, but they are not lost or hidden from God. Isaiah knew that an "ensign to the nations" would be raised to signal the beginning of the return of all twelve tribes of Israel (including the two sons of Joseph: Ephraim and Manasseh). Isaiah prophesied the following:

And he will lift up an ensign to the nations from far, and will hiss unto them from the end of the earth: and, behold, they shall come with speed swiftly: . . . And in that day they shall roar against them like the roaring of the sea: and if one look unto the land, behold darkness and sorrow, and the light is darkened in the heavens thereof. . . . And he shall set up an ensign for the nations, and shall assemble the outcasts of Israel, and gather together the dispersed of Judah from the four corners of the earth. (Isaiah 5:26, 30; 11:12)

The revelation also includes blending Jewish doctrine with the restored truth of Christ, as he taught during his mortal ministry.

From Isaiah to John, the prophets foretell that in the last days, upon the triumphant return of the great Redeemer, all the tribes of the children of Israel will be united in faith and fellowship and will recognize Jesus as the one true Redeemer of the world.

———

NOTES

1. LDS.org, "Brief History of the Scattering of Israel" (pdf), https://www.lds.org/bc/content/shared/content/images/gospel-library/manual/32506/32506_000_057_09-history.pdf. Accessed May 2, 2018.
2. See Bible Hub, Leviticus 26:33, http://biblehub.com/leviticus/26-33.htm. Accessed May 2, 2018.
3. See Bible Gateway, Deuteronomy 8, https://www.biblegateway.com/passage/?search=Deuteronomy+8&version=KJV. Accessed May 2, 2018.
4. Israel in Prophecy, Rabbi Moshe ben Nachman, "The Ten 'Lost' Tribes of Israel and Their Prophesied Return in the Last Days," https://israelinprophecy.wordpress.com/10-tribes/. Accessed May 2, 2018.
5. Jerusalem Center for Public Affairs, Daniel J. Elazar, "The Book of Judges: The Israelite Tribal Federation and It's Discontents," http://www.jcpa.org/dje/articles/judges.htm. Accessed May 2, 2018.
6. Ancient History Encyclopedia, Joshua J. Mark, "Tiglath Pileser III," https://www.ancient.eu/Tiglath_Pileser_III/, June 19, 2014. Accessed May 2, 2018.
7. Encyclopedia Britannica, "Shalmaneser V, King of Assyria and Babylon," https://www.britannica.com/biography/Shalmaneser-V. Accessed May 2, 2018.
8. University College London, Assyrian empire builders, Karen Radner, "Sargon II, king of Assyria (721–705 BC)," http://www.ucl.ac.uk/sargon/essentials/kings/sargonii/. Accessed May 2, 2018.
9. History on the Net, "Assyrian Empire: The Most Powerful Empire in the World," https://www.historyonthenet.com/assyrian-empire-the-most-powerful-empire-in-the-world/. Accessed May 2, 2018.

CHAPTER 15

JUDAH RETURNS TO JERUSALEM

The Lord shall scatter thee.

—Deuteronomy 28:64

Ever hear of the word *diaspora?*[1]

After the Assyrians and Babylonians conquered the northern and southern kingdoms, the people of Israel were dispersed throughout the various lands and kingdoms, either by force or by means of self-preservation and survival. This transformation of the children of Judah is called "the Diaspora," which is the Greek word for "dispersed."

Most of the bloodlines of Israel have been lost through assimilation into other cultures, which came because of their unwillingness to remain true and faithful to the commandments given them by God through his prophets.

While the weak of spirit tend to blame God for their problems, history has shown that disobedience often results in consequences brought on by one's own actions. In 2 Kings and Deuteronomy we read,

> The Lord testified against Israel, and against Judah, by all the prophets, and by all the seers, saying, Turn ye from your evil ways, and keep my commandments and my statutes, according to all the law which I commanded your fathers, and which I sent to you by my servants the prophets. Notwithstanding they would not hear, but hardened their necks, like to the neck of their fathers, that did not believe in the Lord their God. . . . And ye shall be left few in number, whereas ye were as the stars of heaven for multitude; because thou wouldest not obey the voice of the Lord thy God. . . . And the Lord shall scatter thee among all people, from the one end of the earth even unto the other; and there thou shalt serve other gods, which neither thou nor thy fathers have known, even wood and stone. (2 Kings 17:13–14; Deuteronomy 28:62, 64)

When the Assyrians captured the northern kingdom of Israel around 720 BC, after generations of warnings from Elijah, Elisha, and even Moses to repent and leave the ways of the world (which included their idol-worship and following false prophets[2]) and return to God's guidance, the fate of Israel began what would become thousands of years of conflict, captivity, displacement, and diaspora.[3] We again turn to Deuteronomy and read,

> And among these nations shalt thou find no ease, neither shall the sole of thy foot have rest: but the Lord shall give thee there a trembling heart, and failing of eyes, and sorrow of mind: And thy life shall hang in doubt before thee; and thou shalt fear day and night, and shalt have none assurance of thy life. (Deuteronomy 28:65–66)

Israel didn't just break the laws of their people. They violated their covenants with God by worshipping idols and even burning their own children as offerings. The people were ripe for conquest, which came swiftly to most of Israel by the hands of the Assyrians. Within fifty years of the capture of the northern kingdom, however, there was a new tide of power rising in the east. Nebuchadnezzar and his Babylonian Empire moved swiftly against all enemies—including the mighty Assyrians—and swept up what was left of the people of Israel in the southern kingdom of Judah.

With most things relating to God and his children, the promise of redemption was offered, but only after great tribulation and persecution.

Following the assimilation of Israel, scripture offers little reference to what happened to the descendants of Jacob. Although Israel was no longer able to worship in a temple, the Babylonians did preserve a remnant of their heritage by allowing them to assemble and worship as they chose.

Whether because of their humility and return to their core values and faith, or because of some larger plan, the children of Israel were able to return (the first time in a series of comings and goings) to their promised land following Cyrus of Persia's conquest of Babylon in 539 BC. Mentioned in biblical accounts more than twenty times, Cyrus the Great was considered by Jews and historians to be Israel's great liberator.[4] The Lord, through Isaiah, had this to say about him:

> Thus saith the Lord to his anointed, to Cyrus, whose right hand I have holden, to subdue nations before him; and I will loose the loins of kings, to open before him the two leaved gates; and the gates shall not be shut; I will go before thee, and make the crooked places straight: I will break in pieces the gates of brass, and cut in sunder the bars of iron: And I will give thee the treasures of darkness, and hidden riches of secret places, that thou mayest know that I, the Lord, which call thee by thy name, am the God of Israel. (Isaiah 45:1–3)

The return of the remnant of Israel to their former lands included a royal decree to build a temple to the Jewish God, but in the spectrum of time, the occupation of Palestine by Israel's descendants was short-lived. The Jews endured further persecution[5] and subsequent conquests by the Egyptians, Romans, and, in modern times, rogue nations and foreign despots.

Through thousands of years of occupation, persecution, and the atrocities of the Holocaust, Israel has once again returned to its promised land as prophesied by the sages. Whether out of the rising tide of European nationalism born out of two world wars, or by caprice of political upheaval between the Ottoman Empire and Great Britain[6] following a League of Nations mandate that gave Britain authority over the land called "Palestine," the Jewish homeland was reinstated and made sovereign. On May 14, 1948, David Ben-Gurion began his service as Israel's first prime minister and Minister of Defense.[7]

Although the nation of Israel now flies its sovereign flag above its capital city of Jerusalem, its people will continue to be a focal point in the struggle between God's children and the Gentile nations; a struggle that Paul addresses in Hebrews:

> Cast not away therefore your confidence, which hath great recompence of reward. For ye have need of patience, that, after ye have done the will of God, ye might receive the promise. For yet a little while, and he that shall come will come, and will not tarry. (Hebrews 10:35–37)

Notes

1. *Old Testament Student Manual, Kings–Malachi*, "The Persian Empire, the Return of the Jews, and the Diaspora" (Salt Lake City: The Church of Jesus Christ of Latter-day Saints, 1982), 311–16.
2. American Bible Society Resources, "After the Exile: God's People Return to Judea," http://bibleresources.americanbible.org/resource/after-the-exile-gods-people-return-to-judea, Accessed May 2, 2018.
3. Cambridge Dictionary, "Diaspora," https://dictionary.cambridge.org/dictionary/english/diaspora. Accessed May 2, 2018.
4. The Circle of Ancient Iranian Studies (CAIS), Shapour Suren-Pahlav, "Cyrus the Great—The Father and Liberator," http://www.cais-soas.com/CAIS/History/hakhamaneshian/Cyrus-the-great/cyrus_the_great.htm, 1999. Accessed May 2, 2018.
5. ADL, "Anti-Semitism," https://www.adl.org/anti-semitism. Accessed May 2, 2018.
6. Owlcation, John Welford, "British Foreign Policy Regarding the Ottoman Empire in the 19th and 20th Centuries," https://owlcation.com/humanities/British-Foreign-Policy-Regarding-the-Ottoman-Empire-in-the-19th-and-20th-Centuries, April 23, 2017. Accessed May 2, 2018.
7. Jewish Virtual Library, "David Ben-Gurion, 1886–1973," http://www.jewishvirtuallibrary.org/david-ben-gurion. Accessed May 2, 2018.

CHAPTER 16

JEWS CONVERT TO CHRIST

All Israel shall be saved.

—Romans 11:26

Emmah, Tikvah, and Zedakah.

In the Jewish culture, the three principles of "faith," "hope," and "charity"[1] are central to the ancient *Maimonides 13 Principles of Faith*,[2] which are fundamental to every Jewish prayer book and essential to Jewish belief.

Included in the thirteen principles are declarations of faith that "all of the words of the prophets are true" in a restitution and redemption for those who followed God (11), the coming of the Messiah (12), and, ultimately, in a resurrection of the dead (13).

The three pillars of faith, hope, and charity were also central to Judaism's greatest Son—one who fulfilled Maimonides' twelfth and thirteenth principles—the resurrected Jesus Christ. Why, then, is there such a disconnect—almost willfully—between the Jewish faith and the followers of Christ? Will Judaism ever reconcile with Christianity?[3] Some Jewish scholars suggest that Jesus's Apostles, especially Peter, James, and John, never left their faith and remained tied to their Hebrew traditions throughout their lives.

Much of the furor over the prediction of a widespread conversion of the Jews to Christianity surrounds many of the biblical references of a time when Israel would be redeemed, which were made by Jesus and his Apostles.

For the Christian faithful, the words, stories, and admonitions found in the Bible are guidelines for God's interactions and long-term plans for his people. Central to that plan was the state of Israel and its role in bringing to pass the immortality and eternal life of the human race. From Deuteronomy chapter 11:

> For thou art an holy people unto the Lord thy God: the Lord thy God hath chosen
> thee to be a special people unto himself, above all people that are upon the face of the

earth. The Lord did not set his love upon you, nor choose you, because ye were more in number than any people; for ye were the fewest of all people: But because the Lord loved you, and because he would keep the oath which he had sworn unto your fathers, hath the Lord brought you out with a mighty hand, and redeemed you out of the house of bondmen, from the hand of Pharaoh king of Egypt. (Deuteronomy 7:6–8)

But even for his promised children, God had conditions relating to their achieving success in life. Through his prophet he vowed,

If ye hearken to these judgments, and keep, and do them, that the Lord thy God shall keep unto thee the covenant and the mercy which he sware unto thy fathers: And he will love thee, and bless thee, and multiply thee. (Deuteronomy 7:12–13)

Israel, and specifically Jerusalem, was most sacred to the Jews because of its ties to the patriarchs Abraham and David. To Christians, Jerusalem is center stage for the greatest story ever told and was the place where the Savior suffered (in Gethsemane), died (on Golgotha), and was resurrected (from the garden tomb).

The belief in the ideology of "dispensational premillennialism,"[4] which has its roots in the mid-nineteenth century Evangelical movement, hinges on the nation of Israel experiencing a national awakening and subsequent turning to Jesus Christ as a sign of the last days before his imminent return. Ultimately, if such notions are to be believed, the Lord will return, restore Jerusalem, and reign in righteousness as the Apostle Paul writes to the Christian faithful scattered among the Hebrews of Rome:

Behold, the days come, saith the Lord, when I will make a new covenant with the house of Israel and with the house of Judah. . . . For this is the covenant that I will make with the house of Israel after those days, saith the Lord; I will put my laws into their mind, and write them in their hearts: and I will be to them a God, and they shall be to me a people. . . . But Christ being come an high priest of good things to come, by a greater and more perfect tabernacle, not made with hands, that is to say, not of this building. . . . How much more shall the blood of Christ, who through the eternal Spirit offered himself without spot to God, purge your conscience from dead works to serve the living God? . . . So Christ was once offered to bear the sins of many; and unto them that look for him shall he appear the second time without sin unto salvation. (Hebrews 8:8, 10; 9:11, 14, 28)

By way of example, in the Gospel of Matthew, Jesus turns again to one of his favorite parable subjects, the ever-popular olive tree. He refers to the natural versus grafted state of redemption (referencing the world of Gentiles who have been converted or "grafted" into God's favor) and a not-so-subtle reference to his "severity" for those who do not follow in their faith:

Behold therefore the goodness and severity of God: on them which fell, severity; but toward thee, goodness, if thou continue in his goodness: otherwise thou also shalt be cut off. And they also, if they abide not still in unbelief, shall be grafted in: for God is able to graft them in again. For if thou wert cut out of the olive tree which is wild by nature, and wert grafted contrary to nature into a good olive tree: how much more shall these, which be the natural branches, be grafted into their own olive tree? For I would not, brethren, that ye should be ignorant of this mystery, lest ye should be wise in your own conceits; that blindness in part is happened to Israel, until the fulness of the Gentiles be come in. And so all Israel shall be saved. (Romans 11:22–26)

Israel, in Jesus's parable, is again compared to a fig tree whose growth sometimes fades and requires grafting of new branches to stimulate better growth and recovery. As the olive tree begins to blossom once again, he who owns the vineyard will soon come to tend to his garden.

For the Christian faithful throughout the generations of time, the conversion of the Jews has been a much-anticipated sign of the coming of the End of Days and a precursor to the Messianic Age.

Throughout history, Christian contempt for Judaism created levels of mass-hysteria of historical proportions. From the Crusades, cries of "convert or die" became a common segregation point between the true believers and everyone else—especially the Jews. Following the "Blood Purity" ordinance in Toledo, Spain, in which anyone of Jewish descent could not hold public office or benefit from state affairs (and ultimately led to their expulsion from Spain altogether), as well as the Catholic Inquisition of the sixteenth century, even those Jews who converted to Christianity were suspected of dubious intent.

Almost since the end of Christ's ministry and throughout the centuries that have followed, Christianity has anticipated the mass-conversion of the Jewish people to Jesus Christ and their acceptance of him as their Savior and promised Messiah. From Martin Luther to modern-day leaders, the Christian churches have considered the conversion of the Jews a preemptive sign of the return of Jesus. When such a large-scale event will occur, at least according to one prominent Christian leader, is up to the Almighty and no one else. Pope Benedict XVI had this to say about Israel's conversion:

[The conversion of] Israel is in the hands of God, who will save it "as a whole" at the proper time.[5]

Today, Israel is a thriving nation, restored to a stature it has never before experienced. Whether by state edict or by cultural shift, Christianity stands by the core belief that Jesus is the Savior of the world, and that means he's everyone's Savior—Gentile and Jew alike. According to the ancient prophet Zechariah, when Christ does return to stand on the Mount of Olives, those chosen to be with him will be those who will recognize his wounds. He prophesied that

One shall say unto him, what are these wounds in thine hands? Then he shall answer, Those with which I was wounded in the house of my friends. (Zechariah 13:6)

NOTES

1. Israel Revealed, Daniel Rona, "Come unto Christ" (pdf), https://israelrevealed.com/wp
   -content/uploads/BMsummary48.pdf. Accessed May 2, 2018.
2. ORU School of Theology and Missions, "Maimonides' 13 Principles of Jewish Faith,"
   http://web.oru.edu/current_students/class_pages/grtheo/mmankins/drbyhmpg_files
   /GBIB766RabbLit/Chapter9Maimonides13Princ/index.html, chapter 9, 156–63. Accessed
   May 2, 2018.
3. Quora, Daniel Bertles, "Is it possible to reconcile Christianity and Judaism so they are both
   true?" https://www.quora.com/Is-it-possible-to-reconcile-Christianity-and-Judaism-so-they
   -are-both-true. Accessed May 2, 2018.
4. Got Questions, "What is dispensational premillennialism / premillennial dispensationalism?" https://www.gotquestions.org/dispensational-premillennialism.html. Accessed May 2,
   2018.
5. *National Catholic Reporter*, John L. Allen Jr., "Church should not pursue conversion of Jews,
   pope says," https://www.ncronline.org/blogs/ncr-today/church-should-not-pursue
   -conversion-jews-pope-says, March 10, 2011. Accessed May 2, 2018.

CHAPTER 17

LATTER-DAY TEMPLES

In the top of the mountains.

—Isaiah 2:2

Perhaps as early as Adam and Eve, man has been building sacred altars[1] to their God.

A surefire sign of the last days—according to Latter-day Saints' philosophy—is the need for and construction of not one but hundreds of temples to the Lord. In the days of Noah and Moses, God's dwelling place was always described as abiding in the mountains. Many passages in the Old Testament refer to God calling his children from high and holy places such as Ararat, Horeb, Sinai, and Nebo for further discussion, sanctuary, and redemption. In Exodus we read,

> Now Moses kept the flock of Jethro his father in law, the priest of Midian: and he led the flock to the backside of the desert, and came to the mountain of God, even to Horeb. . . . And the Lord came down upon mount Sinai, on the top of the mount: and the Lord called Moses up to the top of the mount; and Moses went up. (Exodus 3:1; 19:20)

The Prophet Isaiah foresaw a time in the spiritual evolution of humanity when the Lord would once again establish holy houses. Isaiah described these houses as being "in the top of the mountains." He prophesied that

> The mountain of the Lord's house shall be established in the top of the mountains, and shall be exalted above the hills; and all nations shall flow unto it. And many people shall go and say, Come ye, and let us go up to the mountain of the Lord, to the house of the God of Jacob; and he will teach us of his ways, and we will walk

in his paths: for out of Zion shall go forth the law, and the word of the Lord from Jerusalem. (Isaiah 2:2–3)

Israel was not exclusive to the notion of temples being erected to God in high positions. From Babylon[2] to Rome, in Buddhist[3] and Hindu cultures,[4] throughout Asia and Africa—even in the United States—high ground has often been seen as a place equated with bringing man closer to his eternal maker. Isaiah writes,

Even them will I bring to my holy mountain, and make them joyful in my house of prayer: their burnt offerings and their sacrifices shall be accepted upon mine altar; for mine house shall be called an house of prayer for all people. (Isaiah 56:7)

Although different in purpose than the original temples of God, which were constructed to pay homage to the eternal provider of sustenance, crops, livestock, land, deliverance, and good health, these modern-day temples are being constructed for the purpose of redeeming the eternal family of man. Apostles Paul and John declared the following:

Else what shall they do which are baptized for the dead, if the dead rise not at all? Why are they then baptized for the dead? . . . I say unto you, the hour is coming, and now is, when the dead shall hear the voice of the Son of God: and they that hear shall live. (1 Corinthians 15:29; John 5:25)

Essential to the redemption of mankind is the acceptance of the purchase Jesus made in the Garden of Gethsemane[5] for the Atonement of each individual living in the past, present, and future, because they cannot fulfill their own salvation without it.

But what of those who never had the chance to hear God's message? How can they know of Christ and his purpose? How can they have the opportunity to participate in the covenants of salvation and the ritual washing (baptism) and redemption by the blood of the Lamb?

One predominant Christian culture's doctrine—the LDS community's mission—is centered around temple work.[6] The idea of performing vicarious baptisms for the dead, as well as other sacred ordinances like eternal marriage, are considered essential tenets of an eternal sealing covenant between a husband and wife and God and have been echoed by various followers of God throughout the ages.[7]

While the Atonement of Jesus Christ[8] assures humanity that each of us will be resurrected and live in some state of eternal form, modern interpretation of scripture, including that of passages found in Isaiah, Ezekiel, and Micah, suggest that temple ordinances are part of the sealing power of God's Eternal Plan for his children. Echoing Isaiah's words, Micah prophesied that

In the last days it shall come to pass, that the mountain of the house of the Lord shall be established in the top of the mountains, and it shall be exalted above the hills; and people shall flow unto it. And many nations shall come, and say, Come, and let us go up to the mountain of the Lord, and to the house of the God of Jacob; and he will teach us of his ways, and we will walk in his paths: for the law shall go forth of Zion, and the word of the Lord from Jerusalem. (Micah 4:1–2)

Modern-day interpretation of the sacred ordinances that were outlined in the early Church suggest that the time has been restored when temples should be constructed to perform vicarious ordinances for those souls who were not able to experience basic gospel tenets for themselves.

The idea of performing mediated work for those who have gone before us has its origins in the Atonement and sacrifice of Jesus himself. When he atoned in Gethsemane and was nailed on the cross, Christian ideology holds that Jesus took upon himself the sins of all mankind—past, present, and future. Thus, his sacrifice of redemption established the precedent for vicarious work.

As Isaiah, Amos, and other prophets have testified of the house of the Lord being established in the mountains, God's people will retreat to those mountains to be further edified under covenant with Him in the last days. Prophets ancient and contemporary foretell of a time when the safest refuge from the rising storms of despair will be (with the exception of a faith-centered home) in God's holy temples, where God, upon the return of the resurrected Savior, will redeem his children. Isaiah prophesied that

In this mountain shall the Lord of hosts make unto all people a feast of fat things, a feast of wines on the lees, of fat things full of marrow, or wines on the lees well refined. . . . He will swallow up death in victory; and the Lord God will wipe away tears from off all faces; and the rebuke of his people shall he take away from off all the earth: for the Lord hath spoken it. And it shall be said in that day, Lo, this is our God; we have waited for him, and he will save us: this is the Lord; we have waited for him, we will be glad and rejoice in his salvation. For in this mountain shall the hand of the Lord rest. (Isaiah 25:6, 8–10)

Notes

1. Sacred Texts, Rutherford H. Platt Jr., "The Forgotten Books of Eden," http://www.sacred-texts.com/bib/fbe/fbe028.htm. Accessed May 2, 2018.
2. Encyclopedia Britannica, "Ziggurat Tower," https://www.britannica.com/technology/ziggurat. Accessed May 2, 2018.
3. Touropia, "10 Amazing Buddhist Monasteries," http://www.touropia.com/amazing-buddhist-monasteries/, October 24, 2017. Accessed May 2, 2018.
4. Wikibooks, "Hinduism/Hindu Temples," https://en.wikibooks.org/wiki/Hinduism/Hindu_Temples. Accessed May 2, 2018.

5. Bible.org, Bob Deffinbaugh, "Luke, the Gospel of the Gentiles: The Garden of Gethsemane (Luke 22:39–46)," https://bible.org/seriespage/garden-gethsemane-luke-2239-46, June 24, 2004. Accessed May 2, 2018.

6. Mormon.org, "What Are Temples?" https://www.mormon.org/beliefs/temples. Accessed May 2, 2018.

7. Jewish Virtual Library, "The Jewish Temples: The First Temple—Solomon's Temple," http://www.jewishvirtuallibrary.org/the-first-temple-solomon-s-temple. Accessed May 2, 2018.

8. Bible.org, Lehman Strauss, "The Atonement of Christ," https://bible.org/article/atonement-Christ, June 2, 2004. Accessed May 2, 2018.

CHAPTER 18

THE LORD COMES TO HIS TEMPLES

I will send my messenger.

—Malachi 3:1

The crowning accomplishment of his reign as King of Israel was Solomon's legacy of completing a temple to his God. In the ancient Hebrew capital city of Jerusalem, Solomon oversaw the construction and dedication of a temple that would become the permanent holding place for the sacred ark of the covenant, thus fulfilling what King David before him had been forbidden to do. 1 Chronicles records the following about David and his son Solomon:

> Then David the king stood up upon his feet, and said, Hear me, my brethren, and my people: As for me, I had in mine heart to build an house of rest for the ark of the covenant of the Lord, and for the footstool of our God, and had made ready for the building: But God said unto me, Thou shalt not build an house for my name, because thou hast been a man of war, and hast shed blood. . . . And of all my sons, (for the Lord hath given me many sons,) he hath chosen Solomon my son to sit upon the throne of the kingdom of the Lord over Israel. (1 Chronicles 28:2–5)

Solomon dedicated lavish resources to the plan for this grand house of the Lord. The ancient Phoenician kingdom of Tyre to the north of Jerusalem provided the cedar for the timbers,[1] and the surrounding mountains and mines provided quarried stone for the edifice itself. In all, more than three thousand teams and respective leaders were appointed to oversee the sacred task, as documented in 1 Kings:[2]

> Then Solomon assembled the elders of Israel, and all the heads of the tribes, the chief of the fathers of the children of Israel, unto king Solomon in Jerusalem, that they might bring up the ark of the covenant of the Lord out of the city of David, which

is Zion. . . . And all the elders of Israel came, and the priests took up the ark. And they brought up the ark of the Lord, and the tabernacle of the congregation, and all the holy vessels that were in the tabernacle, even those did the priests and the Levites bring up. (1 Kings 8:1, 3–4)

This first temple,[3] which was destroyed in 586 BC, was a precursor to what has since become a standard for believers worldwide—in the Christian faith as well as in others—in the common belief that God dwells in holy places.

The second temple, which was built by Israel following their liberation from Babylon, stood for five hundred years until it was destroyed by Rome in AD 70.

It was Malachi, however, who foresaw a time when the Lord would return and dwell in his holy house. He wrote,

Behold, I will send my messenger, and he shall prepare the way before me: and the Lord, whom ye seek, shall suddenly come to his temple, even the messenger of the covenant, whom ye delight in: behold, he shall come, saith the Lord of hosts. (Malachi 3:1)

The holy houses distributed throughout the world, including all related rites and activities, have all but faded from Christianity, with the exception of the Masonic[4] rites and the growing influence of Mormonism as a Christian faith centered on Jesus Christ and his relationship with vicarious work for the dead. Jesus and the house of the Lord have been inextricably connected since he was a child:

And the child grew, and waxed strong in spirit, filled with wisdom: and the grace of God was upon him. . . . And when he was twelve years old, they went up to Jerusalem after the custom of the feast. . . . As they returned, the child Jesus tarried behind in Jerusalem; and Joseph and his mother knew not of it. . . . And it came to pass, that after three days they found him in the temple, sitting in the midst of the doctors, both hearing them, and asking them questions. . . . And all that heard him were astonished at his understanding and answers. (Luke 2:40, 42–43, 46–47)

On the Saturday after Jesus was crucified, his Apostle Peter reported that his master was in the spirit world teaching those legions of souls who had passed through mortality from the time of Noah onward. Peter recorded,

For Christ also hath once suffered for sins, the just for the unjust, that he might bring us to God, being put to death in the flesh, but quickened by the Spirit: By which also he went and preached unto the spirits in prison; Which sometime were disobedient, when once the longsuffering of God waited in the days of Noah, while the ark was a preparing, wherein few, that is, eight souls were saved by water. (1 Peter 3:18–20)

Like everything in the balance of God's eternal plan for his children, Jesus had a task while dead: to preach to those spirits who had not been afforded the chance to hear of his gospel. According to Peter's account:

> For this cause was the gospel preached also to them that are dead, that they might be judged according to men in the flesh, but live according to God in the spirit. . . . For the time is come that judgment must begin at the house of God: and if it first begin at us, what shall the end be of them that obey not the gospel of God? (1 Peter 4:6, 17)

The bible is replete with references to a third temple,[5] but with those references come warnings of a time in which godlessness will follow the sacrifices made there, as in Paul's admonition to the Christian population at Thessalonica:

> Let no man deceive you by any means: for that day shall not come, except there come a falling away first, and that man of sin be revealed, the son of perdition; Who opposeth and exalteth himself above all that is called God, or that is worshipped; so that he as God sitteth in the temple of God, shewing himself that he is God. (2 Thessalonians 2:3–4)

This alleged "man of lawlessness" will, according to Paul, defile the temple by entering it and declaring himself God. As far as the location of this third temple,[6] traditional Christianity suggests it will be reconstructed over the site of one of the previous two edifices, although modern-day prophecy suggests that the new temple will be built by the adopted children of Israel and located in the New World. In his Revelation, however, John describes the triumph of the Savior's return over all lawlessness, especially that caused by the so-called anti-Christ.

The reign of the anti-Christ[7] as a religious and civic figurehead, according to prophecies in John's writings as well as Paul's to the Hebrews, will last for a period of less than four years, in which time he will come to Jerusalem and dwell within the rebuilt temple and act as God Himself. Those who oppose him will be persecuted, since his influence will sway religious, civic, and national leaders to believe that he is God's true mouthpiece. John prophesied,

> Little children, it is the last time: and as ye have heard that antichrist shall come, even now are there many antichrists; whereby we know that it is the last time. . . . Who is a liar but he that denieth that Jesus is the Christ? He is antichrist, that denieth the Father and the Son . . . and every spirit that confesseth not that Jesus Christ is come in the flesh is not of God: and this is that spirit of antichrist, whereof ye have heard that it should come; and even now already is it in the world. . . . For many deceivers are entered into the world, who confess not that Jesus Christ is come in the flesh. This is a deceiver and an antichrist. (1 John 2:18, 22; 4:2–3; 2 John 1:7)

As well as John, the Apostle Paul and the Savior himself prophesied that the defiling of the third temple would occur as a sign of his return. In Matthew, chapter twenty-four, and the second chapter of II Thessalonians, we read,

> When ye therefore shall see the abomination of desolation, spoken of by Daniel the prophet, stand in the holy place, (whoso readeth, let him understand). . . . Let no man deceive you by any means: for that day shall not come, except there come a falling away first, and that man of sin be revealed, the son of perdition; Who opposeth and exalteth himself above all that is called God, or that is worshipped; so that he as God sitteth in the temple of God, shewing himself that he is God. (Matthew 24:15; 2 Thessalonians 2:3–4)

Regardless of whether it will be located in Jerusalem or some other city, the reconstruction of God's holy house is an inevitable sign of the times according to ancient prophecy and modern revelation. The Christian world, however, points to the time when the resurrected Lord—in the flesh—opens the doors of his temple(s) as evidence that God is validating his approval, that Jesus is back, in charge, and quite literally taking names.

———————

NOTES

1. Bible Gateway, 1 Kings 5, https://www.biblegateway.com/passage/?search=1+kings+5&version=KJV. Accessed May 2, 2018.
2. Bible Gateway, 1 Kings 8, https://www.biblegateway.com/passage/?search=1+kngs+8&version=KJV. Accessed May 2, 2018.
3. Jewish Virtual Library, "The Jewish Temples: The First Temple—Solomon's Temple," http://www.jewishvirtuallibrary.org/the-first-temple-solomon-s-temple. Accessed May 2, 2018.
4. Freemason.com, The Grand Lodge of Ohio, "What Is Freemasonry?" http://www.freemason.com/how-to-join/what-is-freemasonry/. Accessed May 2, 2018.
5. ChristianProphecy.org, Lamb & Lion Ministries, Dr. David R. Reagan, "The Third Temple," http://christinprophecy.org/articles/the-third-temple/. Accessed May 2, 2018.
6. EndTime Ministries, Rick Brinegar and Dave Robbins, "Time to Build the Third Temple: The building of the Third Temple on the Temple Mount in Jerusalem," https://www.endtime.com/endtime-magazine-articles/time-build-third-temple/, March 2, 2017. Accessed May 2, 2018.
7. Bible Study Tools, "The Rise of the Antichrist: What/Who is the Antichrist?" https://www.biblestudytools.com/bible-study/topical-studies/the-rise-of-the-antichrist.html, August 22, 2014. Accessed May 2, 2018.

Chapter 19

Persecution of the Faithful

Ye shall be hated of all nations.

—Matthew 24:9

"In God We Trust."

American currency has included this phrase since the days of Abraham Lincoln. With its origins emerging from a national movement to recognize God in some form of national motto, it wasn't until the Cold War that the phrase became an official declaration on all U.S. currency—much to the chagrin of nonbelievers, secularists, and those who just don't want to reference God in any aspect of their lives.

In a distant past, those who believed in God came under such intense scrutiny by those who didn't that the Christian world was almost bled, beaten, and burned out of existence. Jesus warned his Apostles that a time would come when none of his faithful disciples would be safe. He told them,

> Then shall they deliver you up to be afflicted, and shall kill you: and ye shall be hated of all nations for my name's sake. And then shall many be offended, and shall betray one another, and shall hate one another. . . . And because iniquity shall abound, the love of many shall wax cold. (Matthew 24:9–10, 12)

Within thirty years of the death of their leader, the Apostles of Christ had established Christian churches throughout the empire, including Corinth, Galatia, Ephesus, and Philippi. Christian splinter groups had even begun to crop up in the catacombs under Rome itself.

Then came a turn for the worse. Around AD 50, Caesar Claudius decided that Rome should be cleared of non-Roman traditions, and Jews were banished to their own lands.

As discussed previously in chapter 11, in AD 69, about a year before the second temple was destroyed, and four years after the Great Fire of Rome, Roman emperor Vespasian commissioned the great Colosseum, which was to be constructed in the center of the thriving capital. His son Titus later completed the edifice, and its usage as a center for a variety of entertainment has been well documented. During its first year of operation, an average of one person was killed every five minutes around the clock as part of the festivities. These deaths usually occurred from mock battles and executions. The killings spanned almost three hundred years, from AD 64 until the Edict of Milan[1] in 313, when an official proclamation ended the persecution of Christians.

Rome saw that a religious faction was rising out of the Middle East, which threatened to topple even Jupiter himself—the supreme deity of the ancient Romans—with the potential of splitting the empire along cultural lines of loyalty.[2] This did not sit well in the high senate and ruling families of ancient Rome. It was one thing to manage the traditional Jewish subculture, who had been complaining about their oppression for generations. But it was another to consider that a wandering man from the deserts of Galilee could sway even the Jews to rethink their religious position. And thus, the Christian persecution began. Both Jew and Gentile began to follow the words of Jesus as taught by his appointed Apostles:

> [We] labour, working with our own hands: being reviled, we bless; being persecuted, we suffer it. . . . But rejoice, inasmuch as ye are partakers of Christ's sufferings; that, when his glory shall be revealed, ye may be glad also with exceeding joy. . . . Yet if any man suffer as a Christian, let him not be ashamed; but let him glorify God on this behalf. (1 Corinthians 4:12; 1 Peter 4:13, 16)

The Roman Empire was not completely without civility. The three major cities of Rome, Alexandria (in Egypt), and Antioch (in Syria), were social hot spots during the early centuries of the first millennium. They were also large centers of Jewish culture, which had become highly influential in maintaining self-governing control over their territory.

The rising tide of faithful to follow this Jesus of Nazareth did not sit well with the local governments of the Roman Empire or the traditional Jews of the Sanhedrin (the supreme legislative council of the ancient Jews). While the empire was tossing Caesars like a salad (it saw more than a dozen within sixty years), the spreading social and religious ties to the newfound "gospel" began to extend even beyond Rome's borders, as was foretold by Jesus, Peter, and Paul. In his letter to the faithful in Corinth, Paul wrote,

> For we stretch not ourselves beyond our measure, as though we reached not unto you: for we are come as far as to you also in preaching the gospel of Christ. . . . To preach the gospel in the regions beyond you, and not to boast in another man's line of things made ready to our hand. But he that glorieth, let him glory in the Lord. (2 Corinthians 10:14, 16–17)

But the Caesars always had their noses in things, which was the case when the Sanhedrin ordered James the Just thrown from the pinnacle of the temple and clubbed to death. Rome's reaction was swift and firm, resulting in a total occupation of Jerusalem. Roman leadership, it seemed, didn't like uprisings from anyone, even if it was between heretical religious factions opposed to the state religion.

It is said that persecution is a badge of courage in establishing the heritage of those who are faithful to God. Christians were systematically rounded up and executed throughout the three hundred years that followed. Many people who claimed Christianity over Roman customs found themselves entertaining the empire's senators and citizens from inside the Colosseum's walls.

Christians had become an endangered species.

Despite the persecution, however, the Church continued under the authority of Peter, who was given the keys of authority by Jesus prior to his Ascension. Peter held those keys until his death in Rome in AD 66. Subsequent Apostles, including Andronicus, Steven, Barnabas, and even the great Apostle Paul, served as special witnesses of Christ's teaching under the direction of Peter.

By the close of the first century, the holy apostleship under the divine authority granted to them by Christ vanished from the earth. With the last Apostles rounded up and executed, the Church no longer had direct leadership, and many men became self-appointed leaders. Consequently, religious chapters that were organized by the likes of Steven, James, Timothy, and Paul were left to their own designs and influences of the local cultures.

Greek philosophies[3] and other local customs became stronger influences among the Christian factions. By the close of the second century, there were house churches and Christian spin-offs covering almost every major region of the empire. Some efforts were made to keep the foundation of the Church intact, the most notable being that of Ignatius of Antioch[4] in about AD 108, but even his efforts were made while he was on his way to his own execution in Rome.

The Church, as it was organized by Christ and further established by the Apostles throughout the lands, was gone from its original state, and so was its authority. Over the course of the next several centuries, religious factionalism began to creep into the Roman government, and secularism infiltrated the pure Church of God.

For almost two thousand years, the core tenets of Christianity evolved into numerous beliefs, through which emerged powerful voices that led to the establishment of new ideologies and religious majorities, such as the Holy Roman Empire,[5] the Protestant Reformation,[6] the Church of England,[7] and the evangelical revivalists[8] of the mid-nineteenth century in America.

In the 1800s, America was in the throes of domestic political conflict over slave trade, export fees, and land grabbing. A new Christian movement was spreading across New England, but this new Christian sect was different than those migrating from England and Germany.

Young farmer Joseph Smith received a series of visions and was appointed by God to be a prophet. He was assigned the task of restoring what God said would be "the only true and living church." In 1830, The Church of Jesus Christ of Latter-day Saints was established, although the shorter colloquial "Mormons" was attached to its followers.

The Mormons, although rooted in the core beliefs of Christianity, often came under scrutiny by nonbelievers. Historians suggest the sect didn't help their case by segregating themselves away from mainstream American communities, which led to their ouster from various regions in New York, Pennsylvania, and Ohio, often under violent conditions.

Then came Missouri:

> The Mormons must be treated as enemies and must be exterminated or driven from the state, if necessary for the public good.[9] (Missouri Executive Order 44)

In 1838, for the first time in modern history, a legal decree by state order was declared against a Christian group. The decree ordered that they should be driven out of the state and given no quarter. After two decades of wandering and being chased from one town to another because of their non-mainstream religious beliefs, the Mormons found themselves settled along the Mississippi River between Iowa and Illinois. Following further persecution from area townsfolk and the murder of their leaders, the Mormons were forced to leave the boundaries of the United States and settle in the yet unclaimed area that is now Utah.

In a letter published in 1840 in a Pennsylvania newspaper, the Mormon founder and leader of the new Christian sect wrote of his faith as a Christian with a purpose.[10] He said,

> I believe in living a virtuous, upright and holy life before God and feel it my duty to persuade all men in my power to do the same, that they may cease to do evil and learn to do well, and break off their sins by righteousness. (Joseph Smith)[11]

Today, traditional American Christians are finding the notion of living an "upright and holy life before God" even more difficult because of the culture wars and the rise of secularism[12] continuing to change the core values of a new generation. Prayer in schools—even the Pledge of Allegiance—are all but forgotten traits of a former generation. Political pundits on both sides of the argument now find themselves in a struggle for the sake of determining not whether a nation believes "In God We Trust," but whether there is reason to trust anyone at all.

NOTES

1. Encyclopedia Britannica, Roman History, "Edict of Milan," https://www.britannica.com/topic/Edict-of-Milan. Accessed May 2, 2018.
2. Wikipedia, "Persecution of Christians in the Roman Empire," https://en.wikipedia.org/wiki/Persecution_of_Christians_in_the_Roman_Empire. Accessed May 2, 2018.

3. The Gospel Truth, J. W. Jepson, "The Influence of Greek Philosophy on the Development of Christian Theology," https://www.gospeltruth.net/gkphilo.htm, 1999. Accessed May 2, 2018.

4. *Christianity Today*, Christian History, "Ignatius of Antioch," https://www.christianitytoday.com/history/people/martyrs/ignatius-of-antioch.html. Accessed May 2, 2018.

5. History World, Bamber Gascoigne, "History of the Holy Roman Empire," http://www.historyworld.net/wrldhis/PlainTextHistories.asp?historyid=aa35. Accessed May 2, 2018.

6. *National Geographic*, Josep Palau Orta, "How Martin Luther Started a Religious Revolution," https://www.nationalgeographic.com/archaeology-and-history/magazine/2017/09-10/history-martin-luther-religious-revolution/, October 12, 2017. Accessed May 2, 2018.

7. The Church of England, "History of the Church of England," https://www.churchofengland.org/more/media-centre/church-england-glance/history-church-england. Accessed May 2, 2018.

8. Newsmax, "Christian History: Top 5 Religious Movements That Changed America," https://www.newsmax.com/fastfeatures/christian-history/2015/05/07/id/643292/. Accessed May 2, 2018.

9. Archive.org, Missouri Executive Order 44 ("Boggs Extermination Order 44"), https://archive.org/stream/BoggsExterminationOrder44/BoggsExterminationOrder44_djvu.txt. Accessed May 2, 2018.

10. Teachings of the Presidents of the Church: Joseph Smith, "Valiant in the Cause of Christ" (Salt Lake City: The Church of Jesus Christ of Latter-day Saints, 2007), 349–57.

11. Ibid., 352–56.

12. Time.com, Mary Eberstadt, "Regular Christians Are No Longer Welcome in American Culture," http://time.com/4385755/faith-in-america/, June 29, 2016. Accessed May 2, 2018.

CHAPTER 20

PERSECUTION
OF THE JEWS

Wherefore hath the Lord done thus?

—Deuteronomy 29:24

"All the day long" can last for centuries.

From the days of their wanderings in the desert; during their captivity by the Assyrians, Babylonians, and Egyptians; when they were "occupied" by the Roman Empire; and all the way down to the time preceding the twentieth century, the people of Israel have been considered God's collective problem child. As recorded in Deuteronomy, the prophets warned them that

> Thy sons and thy daughters shall be given unto another people, and thine eyes shall look, and fail with longing for them all the day long: and there shall be no might in thine hand. The fruit of thy land, and all thy labours, shall a nation which thou knowest not eat up; and thou shalt be only oppressed and crushed alway. (Deuteronomy 28:32–33)

The persecution of the Jewish nation has been a consistent problem for Israel since the legendary times of Moses, when, after he led the various tribal remnants of Israel out of Egypt, they set the tone for what would be thousands of years of persecution by about every nation throughout the history of the world. God warned them many times that their disobedience, lack of faith, and wanton turning to worldly idols would get them into mortal trouble. In the Bible we read,

> And among these nations shalt thou find no ease, neither shall the sole of thy foot have rest: but the Lord shall give thee there a trembling heart, and failing of eyes, and sorrow of mind. . . . The generation to come of your children that shall rise up after you, and the stranger that shall come from a far land, shall say, when they see the plagues of

that land, and the sicknesses which the Lord hath laid upon it; and that the whole land thereof is brimstone, and salt, and burning. . . . Wherefore hath the Lord done thus unto this land? What meaneth the heat of this great anger? . . . And I will scatter you among the heathen, and will draw out a sword after you: and your land shall be desolate, and your cities waste. (Deuteronomy 28:65; 29:22–24; Leviticus 26:33)

From the mouths of generations of prophets, God warned his children on countless occasions that they would be cast among the peoples of the world if they did not remain faithful to their covenants with him. The Jews were warned repeatedly that they would be dispersed worldwide if they were not faithful to their covenant with God:

But it shall come to pass, if thou wilt not hearken unto the voice of the Lord thy God, to observe to do all his commandments and his statutes which I command thee this day; that all these curses shall come upon thee, and overtake thee: Cursed shalt thou be in the city, and cursed shalt thou be in the field. . . . The Lord shall send upon thee cursing, vexation, and rebuke, in all that thou settest thine hand unto for to do, until thou be destroyed, and until thou perish quickly; because of the wickedness of thy doings, whereby thou hast forsaken me. (Deuteronomy 28:15–16, 20)

The witnesses of Christ's mission and ministry, as documented in the first century in the Greek writings of Apostles Matthew, Mark, Peter, James, John, Paul, and Timothy, were produced and compiled between AD 70 and 130 and became known as the *Novum Testamentum*[1] or "Renewed Covenant." This collected volume of letters and manuscripts became a post-Hebrew-centered treatise on the ideologies surrounding the diaspora and conversion from Judaism to Christianity. It ultimately became a compilation of twenty-seven individual writings put together by Erasmus into a body of work now known as the New Testament.[2]

The dichotomy in cultural awareness, however, was that despite Paul's letters to Christian faithful, as well as to the Hebrews, few people of Jewish faith even knew of the tale of a risen Messiah. As a result, this further perpetuated the speculation by Christians, Hellenists, and Gentiles that not only did the Jews kill their own Savior, but they cared little to learn more about his plan of redemption for them as well.

Europe was no friendlier to the Jewish culture than Rome had been. In the final years of the seventh century, French and Spanish edict forced Jewish families to convert to Catholicism or be enslaved.[3] Such actions from the outside suggest they were based on religious bias between the Christian majority and the Jewish minority. However, historians suggest that the continued persecution of Judaism as a whole was born out of a combination of political, economic, and ideological bias.[4]

For the next thousand years, Judaism was chased throughout Europe as the political target for all sorts of censuring, rancor, and persecution, especially during the period known as the Crusades, when traveling bands of Christian knights would often exercise their superior fighting prowess on Jewish communities[5] along their route to the Holy Land. In Luke we read the following prophecies about the Jews:

And ye shall be betrayed both by parents, and brethren, and kinsfolks, and friends; and some of you shall they cause to be put to death. . . . And when ye shall see Jerusalem compassed with armies, then know that the desolation thereof is nigh. . . . And they shall fall by the edge of the sword, and shall be led away captive into all nations: and Jerusalem shall be trodden down of the Gentiles, until the times of the Gentiles be fulfilled. (Luke 21:16, 20, 24)

Then came the twentieth century.

The region of Austria, Switzerland, and Germany was home to the majority of the house of Israel, who were essentially a people without a country. After the failure of the Weimar Republic,[6] a heavily Jewish-influenced initiative to save Germany from economic ruin in the early 1900s, and a Great War that left more than six million Germans dead or wounded, the nation of Germany fell into a collapsed society that was pinned on a failed monarchy.

Like so many times throughout history, the downtrodden and repressed population of the majority turned their hatred toward a single group. This hatred was based on the failed policies and excessive reparations agreed to in the Treaty of Versailles after World War I. A total economic collapse was looming throughout the hinterland, and even the German middle class found themselves in abject poverty. At this time, the ultra-right-wing fringe of the Nationalist Socialist Party came to power, and a former German Army corporal named Adolph Hitler was appointed chancellor in 1933.[7]

For the Jewish population, their path would be forever altered with the rise of Hitler's Third Reich in Germany and Stalin's Soviet Union to the north and east. Throughout Germany, the Reich ordered segregation between "Aryan" (those who were of pure German descent) and non-Aryan (usually identified as Jews and gypsies). The Nuremberg Laws of 1935 made a formal edict[8] establishing Arianism as a supreme race that must be purged of all outside sources—especially the Jewish influence. Hitler's SS and Gestapo rounded up Jews by the millions, sending them to labor camps and often death by gas chambers in camps that included Auschwitz, Treblinka, and Dachau.

The mass genocide of the Jewish nation became known as the Holocaust. Throughout the period between 1938 and 1945, which began with Germany's "Night of Broken Glass"[9] and ended with the establishment of Israel as a state in 1947, historical records show more than six million Jews were killed[10] under Hitler's orders, while millions more suffered and perished in Stalin's Gulag.[11]

Despite thousands of years of persecution, however, a loving God has promised not to forget or completely forsake his children, as prophesied by Hosea:

For the children of Israel shall abide many days without a king, and without a prince, and without a sacrifice, and without an image, and without an ephod, and without teraphim: Afterward shall the children of Israel return, and seek the Lord their God, and David their king; and shall fear the Lord and his goodness in the latter days. (Hosea 3:4–5)

Today, in a time that some religious historians have proclaimed as the coming to pass of the fullness of the Gentiles,[12] following centuries of persecution, the powerful State of Israel calls to Jews throughout the world to return to ancient lands and take up residence in a long-awaited reunion that Christians have foreseen since John's writings on Patmos. It is a sign that the return[13] of a glorified Jesus Christ is imminent.

Notes

1. Sage Journals, J. K. Elliott, "'Novum Testamentum editum est': The Five-Hundredth Anniversary of Erasmus's New Testament," http://journals.sagepub.com/doi/abs/10.1177/2051677016628242, March 31, 2016. Accessed May 2, 2018.
2. Helsinki.fi, "The Origins of the New Testament," http://www.helsinki.fi/teol/pro/_merenlah/oppimateriaalit/text/english/newtest.htm. Accessed May 2, 2018.
3. Economist.com, Spain and the Jews, "1492 and all that," https://www.economist.com/news/europe/21596963-offer-right-past-wrong-may-not-lead-huge-influx-people-1492-and-all, February 22, 2014. Accessed May 2, 2018.
4. Holocaust Encyclopedia, "Antisemitism," https://www.ushmm.org/wlc/en/article.php?ModuleId=10005175. Accessed May 2, 2018.
5. Chabad.org, Yosef Eisen, "The Bloody Crusades," https://www.chabad.org/library/article_cdo/aid/2617029/jewish/The-Bloody-Crusades.htm. Accessed May 2, 2018.
6. History Channel, "Weimar Republic," https://www.history.com/topics/weimar-republic. Accessed May 2, 2018.
7. History Channel, "Adolf Hitler is named chancellor of Germany," https://www.history.com/this-day-in-history/adolf-hitler-is-named-chancellor-of-germany. Accessed May 2, 2018.
8. Holocaust Encyclopedia, "Anti-Jewish Legislation in Prewar Germany," https://www.ushmm.org/wlc/en/article.php?ModuleId=10005681. Accessed May 2, 2018.
9. Holocaust Encyclopedia, "Kristallnacht," https://www.ushmm.org/wlc/en/article.php?ModuleId=10005201. Accessed May 2, 2018.
10. Holocaust Encyclopedia, "Documenting Numbers of Victims of the Holocaust and Nazi Persecution," https://www.ushmm.org/wlc/en/article.php?ModuleId=10008193. Accessed May 2, 2018.
11. Stanford News Service, Cynthia Haven, "Stalin killed millions. A Stanford historian answers the question, was it genocide?" https://news.stanford.edu/2010/09/23/naimark-stalin-genocide-092310/, September 23, 2010. Accessed May 2, 2018.
12. Signs of the Times, Samuele Bacchiocchi, "Is Modern Israel a Fulfillment of Prophecy?" http://www.signstimes.com/?p=article&a=40044012100.645, January 2010. Accessed May 2, 2018.
13. Truth.net, "Signs of the End-Times," http://www.truthnet.org/Endtimes/introduction/Signs/. Accessed May 2, 2018.

CHAPTER 21

WORLDLY KNOWLEDGE INCREASES

Knowledge shall be increased.

—Daniel 12:4

"I would believe in the concept of Christianity if I didn't know so much."

Whether spoken by a wise man or a fool, intellectual property often fuels the hubris that gets in the way of faith.

For Christianity, one of the many telltale signs of the times relates to a vision experienced by the ancient prophet Daniel:

> There shall be a time of trouble, such as never was since there was a nation even to that same time: and at that time thy people shall be delivered, every one that shall be found written in the book. . . . And they that be wise shall shine as the brightness of the firmament; and they that turn many to righteousness as the stars for ever and ever. But thou, O Daniel, shut up the words, and seal the book, even to the time of the end: many shall run to and fro, and knowledge shall be increased. (Daniel 12:1, 3–4)

Daniel was informed that his prophecy's meaning would be sealed until the time of its fulfillment was near.

From the Stone Age to the Information Age, the evolution of the human race has often been marked by the advancements surrounding the things we use to make life easier. But at what cost?

Christian leaders throughout the world accept that although knowledge and the accumulation of information are growing at an exponential rate, they come at a price. While societies continue to advance in areas of science, principles of technology, medicine, and engineering designs, theologians suggest that a head full of knowledge with an empty heart[1] will lead society closer to the brink of its own destruction. Regarding

Daniel's words, we fast-forward to the Apostle John, who was told in his vision that the time was at hand to reveal his prophecies:

> For the Lord God giveth them light: and they shall reign for ever and ever. And he said unto me, These sayings are faithful and true: and the Lord God of the holy prophets sent his angel to shew unto his servants the things which must shortly be done. Behold, I come quickly: blessed is he that keepeth the sayings of the prophecy of this book. . . . And he saith unto me, Seal not the sayings of the prophecy of this book: for the time is at hand. (Revelation 22:5–7; 10)

While both Daniel and John received similar visions of the time in which "knowledge" (rather than God) would be king, the power of the mind has never been more scrutinized than in our current age of artificial intelligence, fly-by-wire, cyber-profiling, and even Internet dating.

As discussed previously in chapter 1, toward the final decades of the twentieth century, renowned American architect Buckminster Fuller designed what came to be known as the "Knowledge Doubling Curve," in which he observed that human knowledge doubled every one hundred years. He noted that following the close of World War II, the cycle accelerated to every twenty-five years. At present, based on the rate of growth and advancements surrounding the Internet of things, some technologists think we are not far off from the accumulation of knowledge doubling twice in a day's time!

Then there's the debate surrounding the coming of something called a "technological singularity." This is when the invention of artificial hyper-intelligence will inadvertently initiate cascading technological growth, resulting in profound transformation of how artificial intelligence interacts with and ultimately becomes dominant over the human race.

Just how "smart" is the world getting?

- The data contained online now doubles every six months
- Technical knowledge doubles every thirty-six months while printed resources double every eight years
- By the time this book is published, more than half of the one million new titles planned for printing this year will have gone to press.
- There are more than 1.8 billion individual websites[2] and more than three billion Internet users

While Christian scholars infer that the knowledge denoted in Daniel's vision corresponds with that wisdom that comes through the Holy Ghost to discern the mysteries of God, the implied higher knowledge referred to in John's vision pertains to the gospel of Christ and his fulfilling the probation of mankind through the Atonement and Resurrection. John assures God's faithful that

Blessed is he that readeth, and they that hear the words of this prophecy, and keep those things which are written therein: for the time is at hand. . . . And from Jesus Christ, who is the faithful witness, and the first begotten of the dead, and the prince of the kings of the earth. Unto him that loved us, and washed us from our sins in his own blood, and hath made us kings and priests unto God and his Father. . . . Behold, he cometh with clouds; and every eye shall see him, and they also which pierced him: and all kindreds of the earth shall wail because of him. (Revelation 1:3, 5–7)

In a time when the world will generate more knowledge than 57,000 Libraries of Congress within a year's time, some may look at this as a mere humanistic advancement of man's ability to think and reason. They will dismiss this explosive age of knowledge as a mere caprice of evolution. But this is not the case.

A century ago, the horse was faster than the new-fangled automobile that was taking European and American Society by storm. Airplanes were made out of wood and aluminum, and telegraphs were still the preferred means of mass communication.

Today most people have handheld devices that can control every aspect of their lives, send messages anywhere in the world, and store more data than what was used in the early space programs. Man, as was foretold by the Old Testament prophet Amos, has become exceedingly proficient in "wander[ing] from sea to sea, and from the north even to the east," and "they shall run to and fro." (Amos 8:12)

———————

NOTES

1. Countdown to Armageddon, Joseph Candel, "Increased Knowledge," https://countdown.org/en/signs/increased-knowledge/. Accessed May 2, 2018.
2. Internet Live Stats, "Total number of Websites online right now," http://www.internetlivestats.com/total-number-of-websites/. Accessed May 2, 2018.

CHAPTER 22

DISEASE AND PESTILENCE

Fearful sights and great signs.

—Luke 21:11

"Pandemonium."

When English writer John Milton wrote his magnum opus *Paradise Lost* in the mid-seventeenth century, he coined a word that combined the Greek word for "all" (*pan*) and the Latin reference to an evil deity (*daemonium*[1]) to describe the devil's dwelling place.[2]

Today, a similar term—*pandemic*[3]—is used to describe a massive outbreak of disease that spreads rampantly throughout the human race. By consequence, whenever such a pandemic has occurred throughout history, pandemonium usually follows.[4]

While speaking from the Mount of Olives, Jesus pointed to a time when the pandemic of illnesses would burden the people of the earth as a sign of the end of times and his promised return. He warned his Apostles that

> Ye shall hear of wars and rumours of wars: see that ye be not troubled: for all these things must come to pass, but the end is not yet . . . and there shall be famines, and pestilences, and earthquakes, in divers places. All these are the beginning of sorrows. (Matthew 24:6–8)

In Luke we read that the Lord prophesied of a time when, in the last days prior to his return, and in spite of medical developments, mankind would suffer from diseases and pestilences of unimaginable scope and magnitude. The Lord predicted the following about our time:

> Great earthquakes shall be in divers places, and famines, and pestilences; and fearful sights and great signs shall there be from heaven. . . . Men's hearts failing them for

fear, and for looking after those things which are coming on the earth. . . . And then shall they see the Son of man coming in a cloud with power and great glory. (Luke 21:11, 26–27)

In the Apostle John's vision of God's kingdom, he saw four beasts that would be assigned to oversee the woes of mankind. Christian legend holds that the four creatures described in John's vision in Revelation will hold the seals of famine, war, pestilence, and death.

A common visual depiction of one of John's prophecies in Revelation refers to his vision of the four seals of the feared "Horsemen of the Apocalypse."[5] He writes,

When the Lamb opened one of the seals, and I heard, as it were the noise of thunder, one of the four beasts saying, Come and see. And I saw, and behold a white horse: and he that sat on him had a bow; and a crown was given unto him: and he went forth conquering, and to conquer. . . . And there went out another horse that was red: and power was given to him that sat thereon to take peace from the earth. . . . I heard the third beast say, Come and see. And I beheld, and lo a black horse; and he that sat on him had a pair of balances in his hand. . . . And when he had opened the fourth seal, I heard the voice of the fourth beast. . . . And I looked, and behold a pale horse: and his name that sat on him was Death, and Hell followed with him. (Revelation 6:1–2, 4–5, 7–8)

Perhaps one of the more telling signs of the times is the rise of what were once thought to be abolished illnesses,[6] such as the plague, measles, and rubella, not to mention the growing medical concerns surrounding AIDS, opioid abuse, and a variety of exotic illnesses with limited or no apparent countermeasures.

According to medical studies, physicians now advise the public on a regular basis of the resurgence of bacteria that is evolving into drug-resistant strains,[7] including tuberculosis and polio, which were once thought eradicated from society. With the easy access to antibiotics and strong over-the-counter remedies, combined with the driving revenues being exploited by large medical providers, critics suggest that the world is becoming a potential petri dish for powerful new strains of illnesses with the capability of wiping out most of us. The influenza virus, for example, has evolved despite medical attention to evade the human immune system, further establishing the possibility of another global pandemic similar to those from recent history.

Only one hundred years ago, between twenty and fifty million people succumbed to the Spanish Flu,[8] which had a fatality rate of between 15 and 20 percent. Compared with the Spanish Flu of 1918,[9] the current strain of the H7N9 Avian Virus, which has been known to spark into epidemic proportions more frequently than has been expected by medical researchers, has a fatality rate of almost 30 percent. Such a pandemic, some analysts suggest, is more of a matter of "when" rather than "if."

Scientists call attention to the fact that we live in the information age,[10] and the potential impetus for the increase in the risk of a pandemic is due to our trade, travel, and connectivity.[11] Researchers believe that the increased risk of a pandemic of "extinction" is looming in the shadows of medical research despite our efforts to improve on preventive medicine. Each year, more than two hundred strains of cancer,[12] from a combination of factors including heavy elements in our air and exhaust fumes, tobacco, toxic chemicals in food and water, and exposure to the sun, take the lives of more than seven million people.[13] In Revelation chapters 6 and 26, John prophesies,

> And power was given unto them over the fourth part of the earth, to kill with sword, and with hunger, and with death, and with the beasts of the earth. . . . [Then] I heard a great voice out of the temple saying to the seven angels, Go your ways, and pour out the vials of the wrath of God upon the earth. And the first went, and poured out his vial upon the earth; and there fell a noisome and grievous sore upon the men which had the mark of the beast, and upon them which worshipped his image. And the second angel poured out his vial upon the sea; and it became as the blood of a dead man: and every living soul died in the sea. (Revelation 6:8; 16:1–3)

What, then, if anything, should the human race do to prepare for such dire times? Christian leaders, religious scholars,[14] and eschatologists all agree that the countermeasures for surviving such a terrible and inevitable blight on mankind is outlined in more than forty separate exhortations[15] and prophecies throughout the Old and New Testaments. Consider the following reassuring verses in Psalms and Malachi:

> Because thou hast made the Lord, which is my refuge, even the most high, thy habitation; There shall no evil befall thee, neither shall any plague come nigh thy dwelling. . . . But unto you that fear my name shall the Sun of righteousness arise with healing in his wings; and ye shall go forth, and grow up as calves of the stall. (Psalm 91:9–10; Malachi 4:2)

NOTES

1. World of Dictionary, "Daemonium," https://worldofdictionary.com/dict/latin-english/meaning/daemonium. Accessed May 8, 2018.

2. Wordorigins.org, "Pandemonium," http://www.wordorigins.org/index.php/site/pandemonium/. Accessed May 8, 2018.

3. David M. Morens, Gregory K. Folkers, and Anthony S. Fauci, The Journal of Infectious Diseases, "What Is a Pandemic?" Vol. 200, Iss. 7, https://academic.oup.com/jid/article/200/7/1018/903237 (Oxford Academic website, October 1, 2009), 1018–21. Accessed May 8, 2018.

4. The New England Journal of Medicine, Gary W. Small, MD, and Jonathan F. Borus, MD, "Outbreak of Illness in a School Chorus—Toxic Poisoning or Mass Hysteria?" https://www.nejm.org/doi/full/10.1056/NEJM198303173081105. Accessed May 8, 2018.

5. New World Encyclopedia, "Four Horsemen of the Apocalypse," http://www
.newworldencyclopedia.org/entry/Four_Horsemen_of_the_Apocalypse. Accessed
May 8, 2018.

6. Health.com, "5 Old-Time Diseases That Are Making a Comeback," http://www.health
.com/childhood-vaccines/5-old-diseases-that-are-making-a-comeback. Accessed May 8,
2018.

7. Time Health, "4 Diseases Making a Comeback Thanks to Anti-Vaxxers," http://time
.com/27308/4-diseases-making-a-comeback-thanks-to-anti-vaxxers/. Accessed May 8,
2018.

8. History Channel, "Spanish Flu," https://www.history.com/topics/1918-flu-pandemic.
Accessed May 8, 2018.

9. Stanford.edu, Molly Billings, "The Influenza Pandemic of 1918," https://virus.stanford
.edu/uda/, February 2005. Accessed May 8, 2018.

10. The Economist, "From chaos to coherence: Managing pandemics with data," https://
expectexceptional.economist.com/managing-pandemics-with-data.html. Accessed
May 8, 2018.

11. Vox, Julia Belluz, "4 reasons disease outbreaks are erupting around the world," https://
www.vox.com/2016/5/31/11638796/why-there-are-more-infectious-disease-outbreaks,
May 31, 2016. Accessed May 8, 2018.

12. Cancer Research UK, Coping with Cancer, "How can cancer kill you?" http://www
.cancerresearchuk.org/about-cancer/coping/physically/how-can-cancer-kill-you.
Accessed May 8, 2018.

13. WorldCancerDay.org, "World Cancer Day 2013—Global Press Release," http://www
.worldcancerday.org/world-cancer-day-2013-global-press-release. Accessed May 8, 2018.

14. Bible Ministries, "Pestilences—A Sign," http://www.biblelineministries.org/articles/
basearch.php?action=full&mainkey=PESTILENCES+-+A+SIGN. Accessed May 8, 2018.

15. Knowing Jesus, "Plagues," https://bible.knowing-jesus.com/topics/Plagues. Accessed
May 8, 2018.

CHAPTER 23

SCIENTIFIC ADVANCEMENTS

Oppositions of science falsely so called.

—1 Timothy 6:20

The scientific laws surrounding "gravity" are much more complicated than what Isaac Newton postulated in the seventeenth century.

Discoveries expanding how we see the laws of gravity and other physical properties in science required time and the evolution of scientific thought, as well as the advancement of technology and how to apply it to the laws of physics.

Technology and the progression of scientific reasoning in our time have grown expeditiously almost since the beginning of the twentieth century.

One of the significant signs of man closing in on the finish line of his mortal race, eschatologists say, is the advancement of technology and science that will outpace human development itself. For many Christian scholars, the time that Daniel pointed to when "many shall run to and fro, and knowledge shall be increased"[1] is now coming to pass.

Often referred to as the "Father of Experimental Philosophy," Sir Francis Bacon, along with Newton, became instrumental in establishing scientific inductive reasoning[2] as part of the fabric of modern thinking in the seventeenth century. In his epic *Novum Organum,*[3] or "New Instrumentation,"[4] Bacon suggested that ideas about how human knowledge and scientific thought regarding natural and unexplainable phenomena should be classified into empirical groupings based on facts, hypotheses, or an absence of logic.

Bacon's introduction of the scientific method began a three-hundred-year revolution in transforming modern society from a traditionally religious-centered culture to one based on science and logical reasoning for the unexplained. This age of enlightenment[5] produced volumes of writings, new forms of music, refined scientific instrumentation, inventions, and advancements in military science that ultimately led to the nuclear age.

French writer and philosopher Voltaire[6] supposed that the equality of humanity was based exclusively on empirical reasoning. He implied this in *Candide,* his satirical perspective on religious philosophies and excessive living by faith and idealism.[7] A contemporary of Newton, Voltaire believed that it wasn't fate or faith that determined the outcomes of society but the will and reasoning of an inventive mind and looking after one's own domestic follies. In *Candide,* he wrote,

> "It is demonstrable," said he, "that things cannot be otherwise than as they are; for all being created for an end, all is necessarily for the best end. Observe, that the nose has been formed to bear spectacles—thus we have spectacles. Legs are visibly designed for stockings—and we have stockings. Stones were made to be hewn, and to construct castles—therefore my lord has a magnificent castle; for the greatest baron in the province ought to be the best lodged. Pigs were made to be eaten—therefore we eat pork all the year round. Consequently, they who assert that all is well have said a foolish thing, they should have said all is for the best."[8]

Although many prominent minds of the enlightenment period were Christians, the traditional belief system had already begun to change on the heels of the Protestant Reformation, affording new perspectives on how to think about God and his relationship with man (and whether there was even a need to have a belief in a higher deity). Christians suggest that the prophets of old also foresaw this, such as Paul's admonition to one of his principal pupils:

> O Timothy, keep that which is committed to thy trust, avoiding profane and vain babblings, and oppositions of science falsely so called: Which some professing have erred concerning the faith. (1 Timothy 6:20–21)

Through the age of enlightenment, Christians have seen a sort of ironic twist that the matters concerning prayer, divine revelation, and the very life and biblical account surrounding Jesus Christ are considered by some as bordering on the ridiculous. The laws of man, scientists reason, should be governed not by an invisible God but rather through the laws of science.

Today, in a more secularized society than in the past, the notion of science and technology being used to explain away faith appears in almost every aspect of modern life and, some scholars speculate, further make the case of the psalmists, Isaiah, Paul, and others. To the honest in heart, it is obvious that

> The heavens declare the glory of God; and the firmament sheweth his handywork. Day unto day uttereth speech, and night unto night sheweth knowledge. . . . When they knew God, they glorified him not as God, neither were thankful; but became vain in their imaginations, and their foolish heart was darkened. Professing themselves to be wise, they became fools, and changed the glory of the uncorruptible God into an image made like to corruptible man. (Psalm 19:1–2; Romans 1:21–23)

With the mapping of the human genome, chemically-developed test tube babies, cloning, advanced DNA sequencing, and the blending of science and human development, scientific advancement has done much to extend the perception that the laws of nature are the only ones that should warrant thoughtful consideration. Scientific advancements throughout the past 350 years have seen the juxtaposition between human extinction by natural causes and man-made catastrophe, but millions of souls whose faith is not founded in exposure to spiritual experiences are now more inclined to be dismissive of anything relating to God and the mystique that follows the principals of faith and the belief in miracles. In an epistle to the Romans, Paul taught,

> For the invisible things of him from the creation of the world are clearly seen, being understood by the things that are made, even his eternal power and Godhead; so that they are without excuse. (Romans 1:20)

While scholars, historians, Christians, and the public in general would agree that advancements in science and technology have greatly benefitted the human race, the dark side of technology has also led to disasters of epic proportions.

Perhaps one final telling sign of the times that further points to a confluence between technology and prophecy lies in the revelation in which John foresees a period of tribulation that blurs the lines between morality and technology—a time when machines described as "locusts" and "scorpions" will be brought into battle:

> And the shapes of the locusts were like unto horses prepared unto battle; and on their heads were as it were crowns like gold, and their faces were as the faces of men. And they had hair as the hair of women, and their teeth were as the teeth of lions. And they had breastplates, as it were breastplates of iron; and the sound of their wings was as the sound of chariots of many horses running to battle. And they had tails like unto scorpions, and there were stings in their tails: and their power was to hurt men. (Revelation 9:7–10)

Without argument, the study and advancement of science and technology have brought further knowledge, understanding, and inspiration about the human condition and how to improve life as we know it. From such influences as Copernicus and Galileo (who challenged the traditional status quo on the nature of the earth and the sun and their respective relationship to one another) to Charles Darwin and his *Origin of Species*, biology, physics, math, and engineering all point to knowledge being something that evolves in the way that the human race views its existence, well beyond the "Big Bang" that occurred, according to scientists, fourteen billion years ago.

Albert Einstein had this to say about scientific mysteries:

> A knowledge of the existence of something we cannot penetrate, of the manifestations of the profoundest reason and the most radiant beauty—it is this knowledge and this emotion that constitute the truly religious attitude.[9]

NOTES

1. King James Bible Online, "Daniel, Chapter 12," https://www.kingjamesbibleonline.org/1611_Daniel-Chapter-12/. Accessed May 8, 2018.
2. LiveScience, Alina Bradford, "Deductive Reasoning vs. Inductive Reasoning," https://www.livescience.com/21569-deduction-vs-induction.html, July 24, 2017. Accessed May 8, 2018.
3. Study.com, Joshua Sipper, "Novum Organum by Sir Francis Bacon: Summary & Analysis," https://study.com/academy/lesson/novum-organum-by-sir-francis-bacon-summary-analysis.html. Accessed May 8, 2018.
4. Encyclopedia Britannica, "Beconian Method," https://www.britannica.com/science/Baconian-method#ref127745. Accessed May 8, 2018.
5. History Channel, "Enlightenment," https://www.history.com/topics/enlightenment. Accessed May 8, 2018.
6. Stanford Encyclopedia of Philosophy, "Voltaire," https://plato.stanford.edu/entries/voltaire/, July 30, 2015. Accessed May 8, 2018.
7. Encyclopedia Britannica, Sarah Dillon, "Voltaire's Candide," https://www.britannica.com/topic/Candide-by-Voltaire. Accessed May 8, 2018.
8. Project Gutenberg, Voltaire, Candid, https://www.gutenberg.org/files/19942/19942-h/19942-h.htm, November 27, 2006. Accessed May 8, 2018.
9. HuffPost, Krista Tippett, "Albert Einstein's Faith: Was the Great Physicist Spiritual?" https://www.huffingtonpost.com/krista-tippett/albert-einsteins-faith-wa_b_651592.html, May 25, 2011. Accessed May 8, 2018.

CHAPTER 24

ANARCHY, WICKEDNESS, AND VIOLENCE INCREASE

To deceive the nations.[1]

—Revelation 20:8

How do you describe the term "political correctness"[2] to someone?

According to one dictionary definition of the phrase, to be politically correct is to avoid taking a position of extreme exclusion to those who are socially disadvantaged. While liberal thinkers would argue that such a definition would apply to those who have been afforded fewer opportunities than others, Christian conservatives might suggest that "extreme exclusion" and "socially disadvantaged" could apply to any group, depending on their circumstances.

The argument for political correctness would also suggest that taking a bias toward or against any form of governance is offensive—especially in the polarity that often builds between believers and nonbelievers[3] in God and fundamental Christian principles—and, as history has shown, most often leads to chaos, anarchy, and destruction.

Isaiah prophesied that

> The people shall be oppressed, every one by another, and every one by his neighbour: the child shall behave himself proudly against the ancient, and the base against the honourable. . . . The shew of their countenance doth witness against them; and they declare their sin as Sodom, they hide it not. Woe unto their soul! For they have rewarded evil unto themselves. (Isaiah 3:5, 9)

The story of Noah,[4] the Epic of Gilgamesh,[5] and Homer's *Iliad*[6] all frame the chaos of the inherent human condition of distrusting order and discipline, which ultimately leads to a society's destruction.

The authors of Proverbs noted the consequences of a culture left to chaos:

Where no counsel is, the people fall: but in the multitude of counsellors there is safety. (Proverbs 11:14)

Shortly after God established man in his current intelligent form, the wheels of self-destruction quickly started turning, beginning with disobedience, followed by deception, hostility, and moral transgression. From Adam's initial fall from grace[7] following Eve's submission to the adversary[8] and Cain slaying his brother over a sacrificial offering and birthright,[9] to the blossoming and wilting of man, God counseled His children against falling into wickedness, which ultimately fostered a wet reproach by the Almighty. In Genesis we read,

And God saw that the wickedness of man was great in the earth, and that every imagination of the thoughts of his heart was only evil continually. . . . And the Lord said, I will destroy man whom I have created from the face of the earth; both man, and beast, and the creeping thing, and the fowls of the air; for it repenteth me that I have made them. (Genesis 6:5, 7)

Current events suggest that the legacy of calamities surrounding the ancient world are ripe for repeating[10] and have been foretold by almost every prophet from Moses to Paul, including the ancient Prophet Isaiah, who tells us that men shall transgress the law and break the everlasting covenant. He testified that

The earth also is defiled under the inhabitants thereof; because they have transgressed the laws, changed the ordinance, broken the everlasting covenant. Therefore hath the curse devoured the earth, and they that dwell therein are desolate. . . . The city of confusion is broken down: every house is shut up, that no man may come in. . . . In the city is left desolation, and the gate is smitten with destruction. (Isaiah 24:5–6, 10, 12)

Even as this book is being compiled, nations are in full-scale combat dedicated to the utter destruction of Christian-ruled societies,[11] just as was foretold by the prophets, including Paul in his counsel to Timothy:

For men shall be lovers of their own selves, covetous, boasters, proud, blasphemers, disobedient to parents, unthankful, unholy, without natural affection, trucebreakers, false accusers, incontinent, fierce, despisers of those that are good, traitors, heady, highminded, lovers of pleasures more than lovers of God. . . . Evil men and seducers shall wax worse and worse, deceiving, and being deceived. . . . Yea, and all that will live godly in Christ Jesus shall suffer persecution. (2 Timothy 3:2–4, 13, 12; verses not quoted in consecutive order)

Signs of political, civil, and spiritual unrest, especially in the so-called cradle of civilization, have continued almost unending since the times when Israel was led into captivity. Historians, Christian scholars, and social scientists see a continued convergence between what was prophesied and what is coming to pass in Africa and the Middle East in such places as Afghanistan, Iraq, and Syria (all ancient places of corruption and wickedness according to scriptural references). Once again in Isaiah, we read,

> They come from a far country, from the end of heaven, even the Lord, and the weapons of his indignation, to destroy the whole land. . . . And I will cause the arrogancy of the proud to cease, and will lay low the haughtiness of the terrible. . . . Their children also shall be dashed to pieces before their eyes; their houses shall be spoiled, and their wives ravished. (Isaiah 13:5, 11, 16)

Since the latter half of the nineteenth century, in the beginning of what has become known as America's Gilded Age,[12] and loosely corresponding with the advent of the Industrial Revolution,[13] global conflict has seen a steady rise. Over the last century, more than two hundred million people have been killed in various conflicts around the globe, largely due to the corruption of clans, despots, and rogue nations. Peter foresaw these calamities when he stated,

> Them that walk after the flesh in the lust of uncleanness, and despise government. Presumptuous are they, selfwilled, they are not afraid to speak evil of dignities. . . . But these, as natural brute beasts, made to be taken and destroyed, speak evil of the things that they understand not; and shall utterly perish in their own corruption; And shall receive the reward of unrighteousness, as they that count it pleasure to riot in the day time. (2 Peter 2:10, 1–13)

Chaos and corruption are no respecters of persons[14] or status. Signs of turmoil appear on a regular basis across all groups and levels of society. In the modern era of political correctness, scholars might suggest that Christianity has become a socially disadvantaged subset of an otherwise civilized culture, as foretold by the Savior to his Apostles in the Gospel of Matthew:

> For out of the heart proceed evil thoughts, murders, adulteries, fornications, thefts, false witness, blasphemies: These are the things which defile a man. . . . Let them alone: they be blind leaders of the blind. And if the blind lead the blind, both shall fall into the ditch. (Matthew 15:14, 19–20; verses not quoted in consecutive order)

The final days of man's mortality, anarchy, wickedness, and corruption continue to approach the moral boiling point, turning symbolic yellow flags into red ones, setting the stage for something really awful, as echoed in the words of the ancient Prophet Hosea:

> There is no truth, nor mercy, nor knowledge of God in the land. By swearing, and lying, and killing, and stealing, and committing adultery, they break out, and blood toucheth blood. Therefore shall the land mourn, and every one that dwelleth therein shall languish. (Hosea 4:1–3)

Notes

1. See Revelation 20:7–9.
2. Encyclopedia Britannica, Cynthia Roper, "Political correctness (PC)," https://www
.britannica.com/topic/political-correctness. Accessed May 8, 2018.
3. Christ Redeemer Church, The Kingdom Perspective, Don Willeman, "Romans 8 and
the Difference Between a Believer and a Non-Believer," http://christredeemerchurch
.org/home/romans-8-and-the-difference-between-a-believer-and-a-non-believer,
March 3, 2016. Accessed May 8, 2018.
4. Answers in Genesis, "Is Noah's Ark a Myth?" https://answersingenesis.org/noahs-ark
/is-noahs-ark-myth/. Accessed May 8, 2018.
5. Ancient Literature, "Other Ancient Civilizations—Epic of Gilgamesh," http://www
.ancient-literature.com/other_gilgamesh.html. Accessed May 8, 2018.
6. Sparknotes, Homer, "The Iliad," http://www.sparknotes.com/lit/iliad/summary.
Accessed May 8, 2018.
7. The Catholic Faith, "The Fall from Grace," http://www.dacapofoundation.com
/SpecialInterest/DialTheCatholicFaith/Faith&LifeIndex/Level01-5/OKLevelOne5-06
.htm. Accessed May 8, 2018.
8. Bible Gateway, "2 Corinthians 11:3," https://www.biblegateway.com/passage
/?search=2+Corinthians+11%3A3&version=KJV. Accessed May 8, 2018.
9. Bible Study Tools, "Cain and Abel—Bible Story," https://www.biblestudytools.com
/bible-stories/cain-and-abel.html. Accessed May 8, 2018.
10. Faith in the News, Jack Wellman, "5 Bad Ways History Has Repeated Itself," https://
faithinthenews.com/5-bad-ways-history-repeated/. Accessed May 8, 2018.
11. Independent, "Islamic Fundamentalism," https://www.independent.co.uk/topic
/islamic-fundamentalism. Accessed May 8, 2018.
12. The Atlantic, Katie Bacon, "The Dark Side of the Gilded Age," https://www.theatlantic
.com/magazine/archive/2007/06/the-dark-side-of-the-gilded-age/306012/, June 2007.
Accessed May 8, 2018.
13. Financier Worldwide, "Crime and corruption in the 4th industrial revolution," https://
www.financierworldwide.com/crime-and-corruption-in-the-4th-industrial-revolution
/#.WuvhBYgvyiM. Accessed May 8, 2018.
14. The Daily Observer, "No respecter of persons," https://antiguaobserver.com/no-respecter
-of-persons/, April 18, 2011. Accessed May 8, 2018.

CHAPTER 25

WARS AND RUMORS OF WARS

See that ye be not troubled.

—Matthew 24:6

Only a fool would argue against that infamous cliché "War is hell."

Since history was first recorded, the human race has found a reason to hate one another, leading from disagreement to argument, from conflict to combat. The fearful victims are often the innocent bystanders and suffer as collateral damage, while the faithful ask, "Are these the days that are numbered among the stars that fall from heaven?"

While still serving his mortal ministry, Jesus was often asked about the future state of affairs in regard to him and his followers, their community, the world, and the state of the human race. Whenever a conflict has erupted throughout history, Christians often turn to that passage of conversation between Jesus and his disciples: "And ye shall hear of wars and rumours of wars" (Matthew 24:6).

Sociologists suggest that it is human nature to hear and believe[1] only the first part of something spoken, which overshadows anything else that might follow, such as the continuation of this passage in Matthew:

And ye shall hear of wars and rumours of wars: **see that ye be not troubled: for all these things must come to pass, but the end is not yet.** (Matthew 24:6; bold added)

Biblical scholars have frequently debated the suggestion that the intent of Jesus's message and counsel in this verse is often misunderstood.[2] Listing among other future events that foreshadow his return in glory, Jesus included the matter of continued conflict throughout the lands, such as "false Christs" rising up, famines, earthquakes, and what would appear to be unending persecution of his faithful followers. He prophesied that

Nation shall rise against nation, and kingdom against kingdom: and there shall be earthquakes in divers places, and there shall be famines and troubles: these are the beginnings of sorrows . . . and ye shall be brought before rulers and kings for my sake, for a testimony against them. . . . The brother shall betray the brother to death, and the father the son; and children shall rise up against their parents, and shall cause them to be put to death. (Mark 13:8–9, 12)

Catastrophe and perilous times seem to be on the rise[3] across the spectrum of all political and economic factions. While war is inevitable in a world full of varying ideologies, political ambitions, and religions, historians have suggested that modern warfare began with the Civil War in America in 1861 and has continued somewhere in the world up to the civil war in Syria today.

Since World War II, almost two hundred and fifty documented conflicts have been fought throughout a population of between five and eight billion people, with some statistics showing a ratio of ten noncombatant people[4] (those who are not directly involved in a conflict) being killed for every armed combatant. These figures echo Christ's counsel to Matthew, Mark, and the others that is quickly coming to pass:

For in those days shall be affliction, such as was not from the beginning of the creation which God created unto this time, neither shall be. . . . But in those days, after that tribulation, the sun shall be darkened, and the moon shall not give her light, and the stars of heaven shall fall, and the powers that are in heaven shall be shaken. (Mark 13:19, 24–25)

In his words of caution, based on the original Greek text, Jesus was implying that the specter of war will always be present, either in sight or in sound, and that the world, although remaining in a state of unrest, will not fade out of existence. At least, not yet. He forewarned his disciples that

For as the lightning cometh out of the east, and shineth even unto the west; so shall also the coming of the Son of man be. . . . And then shall appear the sign of the Son of man in heaven: and then shall all the tribes of the earth mourn, and they shall see the Son of man coming in the clouds of heaven with power and great glory. (Matthew 24:27, 30)

In an age when world news is fed to every corner of the world twenty-four hours a day, seven days a week, and ratings matter more than truth, the speculation of war, conflict, and all-around bad news[5] does not pass without making at least a handful of headlines on a daily basis. Somewhere—usually in the Middle East and often within cannon fire of ancient biblical sites—the world is always burning. Whether in Iraq or Afghanistan, Somalia or Syria, the sites of ancient battles are the sites of modern conflict. Isaiah described the future in this way:

The burden of Damascus. Behold, Damascus is taken away from being a city, and it shall be a ruinous heap. . . . In that day shall his strong cities be as a forsaken bough, and an uppermost branch, which they left because of the children of Israel: and there shall be desolation. Because thou hast forgotten the God of thy salvation, and hast not been mindful of the rock of thy strength. (Isaiah 17:1, 9–10)

Jesus's half-brother, the Apostle James, identified the origins of war as being born from within the self-turmoil surrounding human worldliness and lustful desires rather than because of society. He declared,

From whence come wars and fightings among you? Come they not hence, even of your lusts that war in your members? Ye lust, and have not: ye kill, and desire to have, and cannot obtain: ye fight and war, yet ye have not, because ye ask not. Ye adulterers and adulteresses, know ye not that the friendship of the world is enmity with God? Whosoever therefore will be a friend of the world is the enemy of God. (James 4:1–2, 4)

According to one group of researchers,[6] the definition of "war" takes on a specific size and shape of conflict:

- War is considered a conflict when the battle death toll exceeds one thousand in a calendar year.
- War is a multi-national armed conflict, which includes two opposing armed groups from external sources of state-funded militaries.
- War may also be considered based on an intra-national conflict between opposing forces within their own border (also referred to as a civil war).

Will war ever cease?

Despite the warnings by apostles, prophets, and the Savior himself, warring factions are expected to intensify as the days between man's hubris and the advent of humility at the coming of our eternal Redeemer come to a close. But throughout the scriptures, in counsel given by Isaiah, Joel, James, Joshua, and Jesus, despite the presence of wars and rumors of wars, those who are faithful as counseled by God's appointed stewards may find peace amidst the storms.

According to James and Paul, it all starts with being kind to our neighbor, staying close to God's witness, and living a peaceable life:

Submit yourselves therefore to God. Resist the devil, and he will flee from you. Draw nigh to God, and he will draw nigh to you. . . . Humble yourselves in the sight of the Lord, and he shall lift you up. . . . I exhort therefore, that, first of all, supplications, prayers, intercessions, and giving of thanks, be made for all men; For kings, and for all that are in authority; that we may lead a quiet and peaceable life in all godliness and honesty. (James 4:7–8, 10; 1 Timothy 2:1–2)

Despite the current state of affairs, which includes hostilities, battles, and bloodshed, Isaiah declared that hope springs not from any power of diplomatic reasoning but from the coming of the Redeemer himself. He counsels,

Let us go up to the mountain of the Lord, to the house of the God of Jacob; and he will teach us of his ways, and we will walk in his paths: for out of Zion shall go forth the law, and the word of the Lord from Jerusalem . . . and they shall beat their swords into plowshares, and their spears into pruninghooks: nation shall not lift up sword against nation, neither shall they learn war any more. (Isaiah 2:3–4)

———

NOTES

1. Lesswrong, Eliezer Yudkowsky, "Do We Believe Everything We're Told?" https://www .lesswrong.com/posts/TiDGXt3WrQwtCdDj3/do-we-believe-everything-we-re-told, October 10, 2007. Accessed May 8, 2018.
2. Got Questions, "What does it mean that there will be wars and rumors of wars before the end times?" https://www.gotquestions.org/wars-and-rumors-of-war.html. Accessed May 8, 2018.
3. Sage Journals, Therése Pettersson and Peter Wallensteen, "Armed conflicts, 1946–2014," http://journals.sagepub.com/doi/full/10.1177/0022343315595927, July 14, 2015. Accessed May 8, 2018.
4. Washington's Blog, "90% of All Deaths in War Are Civilians," http://washingtonsblog .com/2014/05/90-deaths-war-civilians.html, May 16, 2014. Accessed May 8, 2018.
5. BBC Future, Tom Stafford, "Psychology: Why bad news dominates the headlines," http:// www.bbc.com/future/story/20140728-why-is-all-the-news-bad, July 29, 2014. Accessed May 8, 2018.
6. Our World in Data, Max Roser, "War and Peace," https://ourworldindata.org/war-and -peace. Accessed May 8, 2018.

CHAPTER 26

DARKNESS AND RELIGIOUS BIGOTRY

Lest thou be consumed in the iniquity.

—Genesis 19:15

The storm of iniquity, some Christian scholars suggest,[1] is boiling on the horizon. Matters of virtue, self-control, traditional marriage, and the pursuit of what some Christian scholars believe to be a wanton abandonment of all righteousness are being replaced with an "anything goes" way of life. In the Old Testament, the standard for bad living was measured in Sodom and Gomorrah. In Genesis we read,

> And when the morning arose, then the angels hastened Lot, saying, Arise, take thy wife, and thy two daughters, which are here; lest thou be consumed in the iniquity of the city. . . . And it came to pass, when they had brought them forth abroad, that he said, Escape for thy life; look not behind thee, neither stay thou in all the plain; escape to the mountain, lest thou be consumed. (Genesis 19:15, 17)

Many faithful followers of Christ believe that the modern rise in wickedness and the stronger adversarial forces tugging on the righteous are signs of the sunset of the human race.[2] Their position that Satan's growing success is linked to advances in mass-communication is largely founded on the notion that modern technology brings increased corruption.[3] Albert Einstein believed this to be true when he said,

Technological progress is like an axe in the hands of a pathological criminal.[4]

Christians have argued that Satan works to usurp thoughts and emotional responses through the use of easy access,[5] multi-sensory programs and images, popular

120

recordings that not even contemporary artists would describe as music, as well as the excessive stimulus of physical senses.

Christians argue that a common theme in the growing ranks of the desensitized humanistic ideology[6] is the notion that accountability should not have to take a backseat to self-gratification, self-interest, or self-preservation, and the human race can be "good without God."[7]

The current affairs of a world in turmoil include a transition to a more humanistic society in which modesty and conservative viewpoints on God are out-of-fashion with the rise in self-identity, gender neutrality, and political correctness.

Apostasy is the word used to describe the abandoning or denouncement of divine authority. In his counsel to Timothy, the Apostle Paul referred to the last days as being "perilous times." He cautioned Timothy that

> Men shall be lovers of their own selves, covetous, boasters, proud, blasphemers, disobedient to parents, unthankful, unholy, without natural affection, trucebreakers, false accusers, incontinent, fierce, despisers of those that are good, traitors, heady, highminded, lovers of pleasures more than lovers of God; having a form of godliness, but denying the power thereof: from such turn away. (2 Timothy 3:2–5)

Although many people might be unfamiliar with the idea of an apostasy, the cycle of civilizations that have renounced their faith in God has been a recurring scenario throughout history. Some reports indicate an increase in the breach between the once faithful and the newfound cynic.[8] During the time referred to as the antediluvian period, or prior to the Great Flood, the people of Noah's age had abandoned the laws that were established for them by God. As a consequence, they were wiped from the earth. Throughout the many generations since, there have been periods of apostasy in which God's divine direction ceased to be permitted in man's behalf, and darkness fell across the land. Christ warned of this when he declared,

> And as it was in the days of Noe, so shall it be also in the days of the Son of man. . . . Likewise also as it was in the days of Lot. . . . And because iniquity shall abound, the love of many shall wax cold. . . . For then shall be great tribulation, such as was not since the beginning of the world to this time, no, nor ever shall be. (Luke 17:26, 28; Matthew 24:21)

Christians infer Jesus's reference to the times of Noah and Lot, not because of their conducting their day-to-day lives, but because of their abandonment of things holy for things worldly. Further, the Lord suggests that the world will "wax cold" similar to those times as an indication of his imminent triumphant return. His prophetic words were

> And then shall appear the sign of the Son of man in heaven: and then shall all the tribes of the earth mourn, and they shall see the Son of man coming in the clouds of heaven with power and great glory. (Matthew 24:30)

Many religious scholars agree that a Great Apostasy,[9] or falling away from faith, took place following the death of the last of the Apostles of Christ's era. By the end of the first century, the rightful order and sacred ordinances established by Christ through his ordained Apostles vanished from the world. Without the sanctioned governance of an anointed body of leadership, religious historians suggest that the people were left to their own understanding as to what and who to trust regarding the word and will of the Almighty. The Apostle Paul anticipated this when he said to the faithful of Rome:

> And even as they did not like to retain God in their knowledge, God gave them over to a reprobate mind, to do those things which are not convenient; being filled with all unrighteousness, fornication, wickedness, covetousness, maliciousness; full of envy, murder, debate, deceit, malignity; whisperers, backbiters, haters of God. (Romans 1:28–30)

Like his predecessor from an earlier period in history, Paul often counseled as Isaiah did regarding the future state of civilization in which godlessness prevailed. Compare Isaiah's admonitions to Paul's in the following verses:

> Ah sinful nation, a people laden with iniquity, a seed of evildoers, children that are corrupters: they have forsaken the Lord, they have provoked the Holy One of Israel unto anger, they are gone away backward. . . . Evil men and seducers shall wax worse and worse, deceiving, and being deceived. (Isaiah 1:4; 2 Timothy 3:13)

Jesus forewarned his Apostles, as recorded in Matthew, that the world would see a significant increase in wickedness. The ancient writer of Psalm 36 also prophesied this:

> The transgression of the wicked saith within my heart, that there is no fear of God before his eyes. For he flattereth himself in his own eyes, until his iniquity be found to be hateful. The words of his mouth are iniquity and deceit: he hath left off to be wise, and to do good. He deviseth mischief upon his bed; he setteth himself in a way that is not good; he abhorreth not evil. (Psalm 36:1–4)

Sounds like the makings of a gritty movie!

NOTES

1. The Bible Sabbath Association, "The End Time Signs of Increased Wickedness," http://www.biblesabbath.org/bacchiocchi/endtimewickedness.html. Accessed May 8, 2018.
2. The Christian Post, Billy Hallowell, "4 Reasons Many Christians Believe the End Times Are Near," https://www.christianpost.com/news/4-reasons-many-christians-believe-the-end-times-are-near-164280/, May 23, 2016. Accessed May 8, 2018.

3. The Atlantic, Ed Yong, "Corruption Corrupts," https://www.theatlantic.com/science/archive/2016/03/corruption-honesty/472779/, March 9, 2016. Accessed May 8, 2018.

4. Brainy Quote, Albert Einstein Quotes, https://www.brainyquote.com/quotes/albert_einstein_164554. Accessed May 9, 2018.

5. Little Light Studios, "'Knowledge shall be increased,' and so shall Satan's deceptions," https://www.littlelightstudios.tv/knowledge-shall-increased-shall-satans-deceptions, April 15, 2016. Accessed May 8, 2018.

6. Worldview, "Humanist Sociology and Traditional Marriage," https://www.allaboutworldview.org/humanist-sociology-and-traditional-marriage-faq.htm. Accessed May 8, 2018.

7. Reasonable Faith, William Lane Craig, "Can We Be Good without God?" https://www.reasonablefaith.org/writings/popular-writings/existence-nature-of-god/can-we-be-good-without-god/. Accessed May 8, 2018.

8. Billy Graham Evangelistic Association, Billy Graham, "Why Are People Losing Faith in God?" https://billygraham.org/answer/why-are-people-losing-faith-in-god, July 7, 2017. Accessed May 8, 2018.

9. Got Questions, "Will there be a great apostasy / falling away during the end times?" https://www.gotquestions.org/great-apostasy.html. Accessed May 8, 2018.

CHAPTER 27

FALSE CHURCHES ABOUND

That no man deceive you.

—Matthew 24:4

Getting rid of Christians in the first century was all the rage.

The old adage that you shouldn't discuss politics or religion with your friends was no surer than among the halls of Roman leadership after the death of Christ. Management, rule, and expansion of the Roman Empire under the Caesars left little wiggle room for philosophies or beliefs that might have been contrary to the status quo. The Caesars of Rome took less than a century to kill God's anointed leaders, and by the third century, Christianity was a religion practiced only by those who were offered up in the sport of the Flavian Amphitheater—commonly referred to as the Colosseum.

The word "religion" has its origins in the Latin *religio,* which means "something that binds."

Religion in the ancient days, similar to today, was based on a few basic tenets: God spoke to somebody; somebody felt appointed by God to speak to somebody else about God; somebody else told everybody else; and everyone began worshipping God based on the influence, trust, and confidence that the first person or group was in touch with divine authority.

The worship of the Roman gods was not the only popular measure of faith in the empire in the first century. Jewish communities had been part of the Roman fabric for centuries, and eventually it led to a conflict that saw the destruction of the Jewish temple and the further persecution and dissolution of the Jewish culture into numerous religious sects. In AD 66, when the Roman governor of Judea, Florus, slaughtered everyone he could find in the Jewish market for hurling insults at him, a full-scale rebellion of Judea meant legions of Roman soldiers were brought in to fix the problem. In his account, Jewish high priest and chronicler Josephus wrote of the slaughter of forty thousand Jews by Vespasian and his Roman legions:

From one end of Galilee to the other there was an orgy of fire and bloodshed.[1]

From the days of Noah to today, religious factions from all over the spectrum of Christianity have been claiming they were the God's favored fraternity:

And Jesus answered and said unto them, Take heed that no man deceive you. For many shall come in my name, saying, I am Christ; and shall deceive many. . . . And many false prophets shall rise, and shall deceive many. (Matthew 24:4–5, 11)

The notion of independent interpretations of God and his ministry on the earth had become widespread in the first and second centuries. The Apostle Paul, a Hellenist convert to Christianity, dedicated his life and ministry to admonishing the faithful followers of Christ to stay close to the word and doctrine and remain consistent in their practices of keeping the faith. He taught,

For ye are all the children of God by faith in Christ Jesus. . . . There is neither Jew nor Greek, there is neither bond nor free, there is neither male nor female: for ye are all one in Christ Jesus. (Galatians 3:26, 28)

The area surrounding the Mediterranean Sea is massive. The distance between communities in Turkey and Jerusalem was spread over sixteen hundred miles. Today, the drive from Jerusalem and Thessaloniki, Greece, might take thirty hours, given good road conditions and no stops. The journey would take the traveler through five or six different countries and countless communities. Cities along the Mediterranean, however, were dependent on sea travel, and for the Apostle Paul and his various companions—including Luke and Timothy—keeping an eye on the growing Christian faith meant travel by boat to the many communities. Each town, Paul discovered, had its own version of obedience and interpretation of how to live the newfound doctrine of a resurrected Christ; however, Paul's interpretation was consistent with that of the lawgiver himself:

Forasmuch as ye are manifestly declared to be the epistle of Christ ministered by us, written not with ink, but with the Spirit of the living God; not in tables of stone, but in fleshy tables of the heart. . . . Who also hath made us able ministers of the new testament; not of the letter, but of the spirit: for the letter killeth, but the spirit giveth life. (2 Corinthians 3:3, 6)

For the Christian faithful in communities all along the Mediterranean, Paul's thirteen letters to the Christian churches that had quietly cropped up throughout the empire were a way of maintaining consistency amidst the disputing factions. These factions had begun to create their own followings and interpretations of who and what Christ was and his relationship to God and man almost as soon as he was nailed to the cross.

Just as modern communities evolve along unique cultural, social, and even political ideologies from town to town, by the end of the first century, Christian sects had developed independent concepts about what was and was not permitted behavior, prompting what was left of Christ's leadership to embark on those final acts of unification. The Bible records three significant journeys made by Paul. In these journeys, he encountered a variety of churches, all of which had drifted into their own individual sets of beliefs and tribulations.

While it is considered a fact that Paul wrote thirteen letters to the various Christian churches, scholars still debate on whether he was the author of Hebrews.

In all, the various chapters of Christianity included many towns and congregations, each with their own ideologies. While not a definitive list, the following suggests some of the major populations where Christianity found itself in one form or another mingled with the local traditions and customs. These areas were center to Paul's three missionary journeys:

- Jerusalem—Three distinct groups of Jews (Palestinians,[2] Rabbinics,[3] and Hellenists[4]).

- Rome[5]—In the first century, Roman religion was a house-to-house principle that centered around whoever was the traditional god worshipped by the paterfamilias.

- Samaria[6]—Opposed repatriation of Judah to the northern lands. They called themselves the "Keepers of the Torah."

- Caesarea[7]—Blended Roman polytheism with Jewish hard-liners who were killed for their faith

- Antioch[8]—The first reference to followers of Jesus as "Christians," the so-called "Followers of the Way" were the first Gentile converts to organize into a congregation.

- Cyprus[9]—Greek religious castaways that congregated and worshipped in caves. They were taught how to worship by Barnabas.

- Iconium[10]—Greek-Asian influence blended with Judaism.

- Laodicea[11]—(Collose): The last of the seven churches referenced by John in his Revelation. A student of Paul's allegedly organized the faithful there. Their congregations loved their wealth more than God and followed dynastic rule and traditional Roman myth.

- Miletus[12]—Ancient Indo-Asian city that practiced various perverted forms of paganism mingled with Christian fundamentals.

- Ephesus[13]—Worshipped the resident "Mother Goddess Artemis" and a blend of Jewish influence with Gentile converts.

- Troas—A port city on the Aegean Sea, popular for Roman cult following, paganism, and typical port-side debauchery of the times.

- Assos[14]—A city of intellects, where logic and facts superseded the notion of a risen Messiah. Assos was the birthplace and home of the school founded by ancient philosopher Aristotle.

- Philippi[15]—A Roman stronghold with its own gold mine. It included a large population of Italian immigrants.

- Athens[16]—Classified as a "free city" by the Empire, Athens was heavily influenced by traditional Greek polytheism.

- Corinth[17]—Also influenced by Greece's Olympian gods, which included what Christian scholars often refer to as "moral corruption."[18]

- Thessalonica[19]—An ancient port city whose local congregations mixed their new Christian faith with traditional immoral practices of mysticism tied to idols ("Cabiri"[20]).

The formal religion of ancient Romans[21] was all about binding families to households, binding households to the male dominant figure, and binding him to his favorite deity. Such was the way of Roman worship, and it was indisputable.

By the beginning of the fourth century, Rome became so large that by the Emperor Diocletian's edict, four lesser kings assisted the empire in holding off the barbarian hordes from the north (the Goths, Vandals, etc.). The tetrarchy,[22] as it was known, was not successful, and within a few years, everybody wanted to be the sole leader over the vast Mediterranean empire.

Also by the beginning of the fourth century, the military campaigns of Constantine resulted in unifying the four regions of the empire that had been divided into lesser realms. As discussed previously, Constantine, a man whose mother had converted to Christianity, was the first Roman emperor to declare Christianity absolved from further exploit and persecution. He also embraced it as the state religion. In 324, when he moved the seat of the empire to a port town near the mouth of the Black Sea, where traditional Eastern Europe meets West, the ancient city of Byzantium was renamed Constantinople, and the seeds of what would become the great schism between Greek Orthodox and Roman Catholicism were planted.

Today more than forty-three hundred different religions are practiced in the world,[23] with more than thirty-three thousand independent Christian sects, no doubt fulfilling a common theme among the Lord and his followers about the last days. In his first epistle, the Apostle John wrote,

> Beloved, believe not every spirit, but try the spirits whether they are of God: because many false prophets are gone out into the world. . . . Every spirit that confesseth that

Jesus Christ is come in the flesh is of God: And every spirit that confesseth not that Jesus Christ is come in the flesh is not of God: and this is that spirit of antichrist, whereof ye have heard that it should come; and even now already is it in the world. (1 John 4:1–3)

Fortunately for the faithful of Christ, Paul, in his letter to the Christians in Corinth, testified that God is not a God of confusion. He wrote,

For God is not the author of confusion, but of peace, as in all churches of the saints. (1 Corinthians 14:33)

———

NOTES

1. The Jewish Magazine, Norman A. Rubin, "The Great Revolt in the Galilee," http://www
.jewishmag.com/176mag/revolt_in_galilee/revolt_in_galilee.htm. Accessed May 8, 2018.
2. The Atlantic, H. Sacher, "A Jewish Palestine," https://www.theatlantic.com/magazine
/archive/1919/07/a-jewish-palestine/303393/, July 1919. Accessed May 8, 2018.
3. The Gospel Coalition, Joe Carter, "9 Things You Should Know about Rabbinic Judaism,"
https://www.thegospelcoalition.org/article/9-things-you-should-know-about-rabbinic
-judaism/, August 26, 2014. Accessed May 8, 2018.
4. Jewish Encyclopedia, Carl Siegfried and Richard Gottheil, "Hellenism," http://www
.jewishencyclopedia.com/articles/7535-hellenism. Accessed May 8, 2018.
5. Emma Johnson, "Patriarchal Power in the Roman Republic: Ideologies and Realities of
the Paterfamilias," http://www.mcgill.ca/classics/files/classics/2006-7-07.pdf. Accessed
May 8, 2018.
6. Bible.ca, Steve Rudd, "The Samaritans," http://www.bible.ca/archeology/bible-archeology
-samaritans.htm, 2006. Accessed May 8, 2018.
7. Encyclopedia Britannica, "Caesarea, Ancient City, Israel," https://www.britannica.com
/place/Caesarea. Accessed May 8, 2018.
8. Ligonier Ministries, "The Church in Antioch," https://www.ligonier.org/learn/devotionals
/the-church-in-antioch/. Accessed May 8, 2018.
9. Ring of Christ, "The Early Christian History of Cyprus to the 5th Century," http://
ringofchrist.com/early-christian-history/. Accessed May 8, 2018.
10. Biblestudy.org, "Iconium, Lystra, and Derbe," http://www.biblestudy.org/apostlepaul
/life-epistles-of-apostle-paul/iconium-lystra-derbe.html. Accessed May 8, 2018.
11. Bible History Daily, Megan Sauter, "The Church of Laodicea in the Bible and
Archaeology," https://www.biblicalarchaeology.org/daily/biblical-sites-places/biblical
-archaeology-sites/church-of-laodicea-in-the-bible-and-archaeology/, March 6, 2017.
Accessed May 8, 2018.
12. ThoughtCo., N. S. Gill, "Miletus, Origins of the Greek Colony," https://www.thoughtco
.com/miletus-greek-history-119714, March 8, 2017. Accessed May 8, 2018.
13. Ancient History Encyclopedia, Joshua J. Mark, "Ephesus," https://www.ancient.eu
/ephesos/, September 2, 2009. Accessed May 8, 2018.

14. Bible Atlas, Bible Hub, "Assos," http://bibleatlas.org/assos.htm. Accessed May 8, 2018.

15. Ancient History Encyclopedia, Mark Cartwright, "Philippi," https://www.ancient.eu /Philippi/, May 4, 2016. Accessed May 8, 2018.

16. Ancient History Encyclopedia, Mark Cartwright, "Ancient Greek Religion," https:// www.ancient.eu/Greek_Religion/, March 13, 2018. Accessed May 8, 2018.

17. Bible Atlas, Bible Hub, "Corinth," http://bibleatlas.org/corinth.htm. Accessed May 8, 2018.

18. The Baker Deep End Blog, Louis, "How Immoral Was the City of Corinth—Really?" https://bbhchurchconnection.wordpress.com/2015/01/09/how-immoral-was-corinth -really/, January 9, 2015. Accessed May 8, 2018.

19. Bible Study Tools, "The Church of Thessalonica," https://www.biblestudytools.com /history/joseph-barber-lightfoot-biblical-essays/the-church-of-thessalonica.html. Accessed May 8, 2018.

20. Encyclopedia.com, "Cabiri (Or Cabeiri)," https://www.encyclopedia.com/philosophy -and-religion/ancient-religions/ancient-religion/cabiri. Accessed May 8, 2018.

21. Ancient History Encyclopedia, Donald L. Wasson, "Roman Religion," https:// www.ancient.eu/Roman_Religion/, November 13, 2013. Accessed May 8, 2018.

22. Lumen Learning, ER Services, Western Civilization, "Diocletian and the Tetrarchy," https://courses.lumenlearning.com/suny-hccc-worldhistory/chapter/diocletian-and-the -tetrarchy/. Accessed May 8, 2018.

23. The Register, Stephen Juan, "What are the most widely practiced religions of the world?" https://www.theregister.co.uk/2006/10/06/the_odd_body_religion/, October 6, 2006. Accessed May 8, 2018.

Chapter 28

Men Refuse to Believe the Signs of the Times

Can ye not discern the signs?

—Matthew 16:3

I f the reassurance of a world devastated and overcome by fire and damnation doesn't pose enough incentive for the human race to call itself to some higher form of spiritual order, Paul also reminds us that there are no second chances after death:

> I have heard thee in a time accepted, and in the day of salvation have I succoured thee: behold, now is the accepted time; behold, now is the day of salvation. (2 Corinthians 6:2)

In his many letters to the budding body of the Church of Christ, Paul reminded those from myriad backgrounds and scores of tongues and traditions that just as Jesus lived one life to atone for the human race, so shall all of us only get one chance at mortality. He proclaimed,

> But now once in the end of the world hath he appeared to put away sin by the sacrifice of himself. And as it is appointed unto men once to die, but after this the judgment: So Christ was once offered to bear the sins of many; and unto them that look for him shall he appear the second time without sin unto salvation. (Hebrews 9:26–28)

Just as there will be readers of this work who will speculate, conjecture, and criticize what has been offered as merely one writer's perspectives on the threads of eschatology, so too have there always been cynics who have chosen to deny the signs of the times. In the time of ancient Israel, even in the presence of great miracles and the appearances of angels, God's children often doubted the signs of the times:

> Therefore the people came to Moses, and said, We have sinned, for we have spoken against the Lord, and against thee; pray unto the Lord, that he take away the serpents from us. . . . And Moses made a serpent of brass, and put it upon a pole, and it came to pass, that if a serpent had bitten any man, when he beheld the serpent of brass, he lived. (Numbers 21:7, 9)

Time and again, despite examples and warnings, mankind has had a problem believing what we read, hear about, and even see. In the case of the so-called "brazen serpent" on top of Moses's staff, it, rather than the faith it represented, became an object of worship that Judah's righteous king Hezekiah destroyed five hundred years later. In 2 Kings we read,

> Hezekiah the son of Ahaz king of Judah began to reign. . . . And he did that which was right in the sight of the Lord, according to all that David his father did. He removed the high places, and brake the images, and cut down the groves, and brake in pieces the brasen serpent that Moses had made: for unto those days the children of Israel did burn incense to it: and he called it Nehushtan. (2 Kings 18:1, 3–4)

The Bible offers many examples of ancient times when those chosen to do God's work were abandoned, abused, persecuted, and put to death despite the signs. One of the most outspoken prophets of his time, Isaiah foretold of a coming Redeemer who would save the world from itself:

- Heaven will give the sign of a babe being born to a virgin (7:14).
- His heritage will come through the house of David (9:7).
- His way will be prepared before him (by John the Baptist—his cousin) (40:3).
- He will make a blood atonement (53:5).
- He will bear the sins and sorrows of all of us (53:4).
- He will be buried in the tomb of a wealthy man (53:9).
- He will judge the world in righteousness (11:4).

Yet, despite the promptings of a great prophet, as well as the forewarnings of those who followed Isaiah, the children of Israel continued to ignore the signs given them.

During his encounter with the Pharisees, Jesus reproached them for not identifying the biblical signs that had foreshadowed the times they were living in, and he chastised them for it:

> He answered and said unto them, When it is evening, ye say, It will be fair weather: for the sky is red. And in the morning, It will be foul weather to day: for the sky is red and lowring. O ye hypocrites, ye can discern the face of the sky; but can ye not discern the signs of the times? (Matthew 16:2–3)

While the Pharisees and Sadducees were attempting to trap Jesus in a double-jeopardy compromise (like generations before them), Jesus used the analogy of the weather to predict the coming of difficult times. As in Noah's time, although from God's viewpoint and that of his faithful followers, the impending storm clouds heralded the coming rains that consumed just about everyone. But the people, like the Pharisees and Sadducees, ignored the warnings. Jesus cautioned his disciples that

> As in the days that were before the flood they were eating and drinking, marrying and giving in marriage, until the day that Noe entered into the ark, and knew not until the flood came, and took them all away; so shall also the coming of the Son of man be. (Matthew 24:38–39)

Like the many prophets who were sent by his Father before him, Jesus made extra effort to warn even his enemies of the impending time of their demise. In what has become known throughout the Christian world as the Olivet Prophecy, Jesus foretold of a time when the temple would be destroyed, his followers would be persecuted for his name's sake, and—like the surety of the temple being rebuilt in the last days—he would be resurrected and eventually return in glory:

> And Jesus answering said unto him, Seest thou these great buildings? There shall not be left one stone upon another, that shall not be thrown down. . . . And the gospel must first be published among all nations. . . . For false Christs and false prophets shall rise, and shall shew signs and wonders, to seduce, if it were possible, even the elect. . . . Take heed that no man deceive you. For many shall come in my name, saying, I am Christ; and shall deceive many. . . . And many false prophets shall rise, and shall deceive many. And because iniquity shall abound, the love of many shall wax cold. . . . Settle it therefore in your hearts, not to meditate before what ye shall answer: For I will give you a mouth and wisdom, which all your adversaries shall not be able to gainsay nor resist. . . . And ye shall be hated of all men for my name's sake. . . . But in those days, after that tribulation, the sun shall be darkened, and the moon shall not give her light, and the stars of heaven

shall fall, and the powers that are in heaven shall be shaken. And then shall they see the Son of man coming in the clouds with great power and glory. (Mark 13:2, 10, 22, 24–26; Matthew 24:4–5, 11–12; Luke 21:14–15, 17; verses not in consecutive order)

Another of his poignant prophecies was that his gospel would be preached throughout the world before he would return. He testified that

This gospel of the kingdom shall be preached in all the world for a witness unto all nations; and then shall the end come. (Matthew 24:14)

Among the 195 countries of the world and the seven billion people who live here, the Christian population has quadrupled[1] over the past century alone. Currently, more than two billion people claim some form of Christian principle as a core tenet of their religion. While the entire Western Hemisphere is predominantly Christian,[2] the spread of the word of Christ throughout southern and central Africa, Eastern Europe, and Northern Asia are seeing steady increases in those who believe in the story of Jesus and his ministry.

The long, dark journey of Christianity from the time of Peter, James, John, Paul, and Jesus up to our day has been ripe with signs of turmoil, tribulation, adversity, nobility, and triumph.

At the conclusion of his counsel to his Apostles from the Mount of Olives, and shortly before he retreated to a nearby garden to atone for the sins of the human race, Jesus offered a warning and loving advice for those who would believe in his mission, and his words are the best way to conclude this section:

Heaven and earth shall pass away: but my words shall not pass away. And take heed to yourselves, lest at any time your hearts be overcharged with surfeiting, and drunkenness, and cares of this life, and so that day come upon you unawares. For as a snare shall it come on all them that dwell on the face of the whole earth. Watch ye therefore, and pray always, that ye may be accounted worthy to escape all these things that shall come to pass, and to stand before the Son of man. (Luke 21:34–36)

Notes

1. Pew Research Center, "Global Christianity—A Report on the Size and Distribution of the World's Christian Population," http://www.pewforum org/2011/12/19/global-christianity-exec/, December 19, 2011. Accessed May 8, 2018.

2. *The Washington Post*, Max Fisher, "Our Christian Earth: The astounding reach of the world's largest religion, in charts and maps," https://www.washingtonpost .com/news/worldviews/wp/2012/12/18/our-christian-earth-the-astounding -reach-of-the-worlds-largest-religion-in-charts-and-maps, December 18, 2012. Accessed May 8, 2018.

PART IV

FORESHADOWING THE INEVITABLE

Christus nobiscum est usque ad consummationem mundi!

Christ is with us until the world's end![1] (William Tyndale)

Rounding out our journey with this concluding section, these last five chapters explore the final foreshadowing of man's closing days. Again, turning to biblical references, this section discusses how man might be heading on a collision course with his own self-inflicted destiny (or demise).

Perhaps one of the most misunderstood concepts of Christianity is the notion that the "Apocalypse"[2] means the end of all life as we know it. Many religious cultures believe that the final dispensation of mankind and the ultimate return of the Savior will herald the apocalypse (in this context meaning the end of the world). However, the word *apocalypse* is a Greek word that means "revelation," and the term connotes anything that is revealed about future events as a matter of general principle.

For example, if someone were to profess that the Utah Jazz would ever win an NBA championship, that would be considered an apocalyptic statement. And, by the way, such an event would in no way coincide with hell freezing over (which would be another apocalyptic statement).

But when will the End of Days actually occur?

As discussed in part two of this book, some scholars suggest that the end has already begun and that in its 4.5 billion years since its origins, the earth itself is living on borrowed time.[3] Over the course of the past 500 million years, based on scientists' reports, the earth has experienced many "extinction-level" events, including the Ordovician,[4] Devonian,[5] Permian,[6] Jurassic,[7] and Cretaceous[8] extinctions. What do we, as a species, have to say about or do with our own mortality? Is man helping or hindering his own tenure on the earth?

In Matthew's account, Jesus refers to the imminent End of Days. He declares,

For many shall come in my name, saying, I am Christ; and shall deceive many. And ye shall hear of wars and rumours of wars: see that ye be not troubled: for all these things must come to pass, but the end is not yet. For nation shall rise against nation, and kingdom against kingdom: and there shall be famines, and pestilences, and earthquakes, in divers places (Matthew 24:5–7).

In the end, and regardless of what man's final "period" may be called by future historians, who wins and who loses and how long we lasted may not be a surprise to anyone—especially those who have stayed close to the signs of the times and understand their part in what Latter-day Saints call "the plan."

————

NOTES

1. Christian Today, Mark Woods, "William Tyndale: 10 Quotes from the Martyr Burned for Translating Scripture," https://www.christiantoday.com/article/william.tyndale.10.quotes.from.the.martyr.burned.for.translating.scripture/97290.htm, October 6, 2016. Accessed April 25, 2018.
2. History Channel, "Religions on the End of the World," http://www.history.com/topics/religions-on-the-end-of-the-world. Accessed April 25, 2018.
3. University of Washington News, Sandra Hines, "'The end of the world' has already begun, UW Scientists Say," http://www.washington.edu/news/2003/01/13/the-end-of-the-world-has-already-begun-uw-scientists-say/, January 13, 2013. Accessed April 25, 2018.
4. National Geographic Science, Prehistoric World, "Ordovician Period," https://www.nationalgeographic.com/science/prehistoric-world/ordovician/. Accessed April 25, 2018.
5. Encyclopedia Britannica, Michael R. House, "Devonian Period," https://www.britannica.com/science/Devonian-Period. Accessed April 25, 2018.
6. National Geographic Science, Prehistoric World, "Permian Period," https://www.nationalgeographic.com/science/prehistoric-world/permian/. Accessed April 25, 2018.
7. National Geographic Science, Prehistoric World, "Jurassic Period," https://www.nationalgeographic.com/science/prehistoric-world/jurassic/. Accessed April 25, 2018.
8. Sam Noble Museum, "End-Cretaceous Extinction," http://samnoblemuseum.ou.edu/understanding-extinction/mass-extinctions/end-cretaceous-extinction/. Accessed April 25, 2018.

CHAPTER 29

WONDERS IN THE HEAVENS AND ON THE EARTH

The day of the Lord cometh.

—Joel 2:1

Many Christian faiths teach of a "rapture." Rapture is a word invented by British evangelist John Nelson Darby, the so-called "Father of Dispensationalism."[1] The word is based on an interpretation of 1 Thessalonians about the righteous followers of Jesus being "carried away in the clouds."[2] These faiths believe that those who accepted Christ as their savior will immediately vanish from the world or be carried up into heaven when he returns.

While some Christian believers teach of a time when the righteous will be called up to meet Jesus before he cleanses the world with fire, other Christian sects take attention to detail one step farther. They believe there's more to getting that spiritual ticket to ride with Christ than just admitting he's the Messiah. (And it's highly unlikely that there will be any trip up into the clouds as Paul's words are often interpreted to mean.)

The "Millennium"[3] is the period of time that the LDS faithful say represents the thousand years following the return of Christ. It is frequently used as the general reference point of the final period before the last Judgment, and that—as foretold by the prophets of old—will be heralded by earthquakes, giant storms, fire in the sky, and wars and rumors of wars. (Sounds like last week's headlines!)

For more than two thousand years, legend, prophecies, oracles, and even astronomers have deliberated on the notion that the clock is winding down on mortality. Ask ten different people from ten different Christian faiths, and chances are there will be ten different perspectives all rooted in some sense of "doctrine" as to the coming of that "great and dreadful day" or the Second Coming of Christ. Throughout history, books have been written, movies produced, and songs have been sung about the Millennium[4]—along with plenty of wailing and gnashing of teeth over false alarms. From a pure sense of biblical scholarship, as recorded by John in Revelation 20, the

Millennium describes that period when Satan is bound during the thousand-year resurrected ministry of Christ[5] on earth. John wrote,

> And I saw an angel come down from heaven, having the key of the bottomless pit and a great chain in his hand. And he laid hold on the dragon, that old serpent, which is the Devil, and Satan, and bound him a thousand years, and cast him into the bottomless pit, and shut him up, and set a seal upon him, that he should deceive the nations no more, till the thousand years should be fulfilled: and after that he must be loosed a little season. (Revelation 20:1–3)

As discussed in chapter 7, to Christians, the Epiphany, or epiphanaeia,[6] represents the return or "appearance" of Christ in his glory. But Judaism contends that the whole idea of a "Second Coming" is little more than a ruse contrived by dissatisfied Christians (and displaced Jews).

Everyone seems to have an insider track on the ultimate Christian events corresponding with the Second Coming of Christ. Just after AD 1000, religious radicals throughout Medieval Europe were so convinced that the End of Days was upon them that some of the more zealous of the followers flung themselves from mountaintops, thinking their offering would be sufficient compensation for their misdeeds in life. Others walled themselves into caves and stopped talking and eating for as long as they could before succumbing to fatigue, insanity, or death. Christians surrendered their earthly belongings to the church, anticipating that their penance (and meager offerings) would benefit them upon the Lord's return. Given the lack of education about the actual date and time from day to day, most faithful followers had no idea what day or year it was and remained unaffected at the passing of the first millennium. Conversely, as time passed (and the resurrected Jesus was nowhere to be found), the church offered no refunds on those possessions given.

The coming of the so-called last days, however, was prophesied many hundreds of years before the first millennium. Around the year 750 BC, back when King Uzziah was leading the Kingdom of Judah to more than fifty years of innovation and political advancement, the Prophet Amos wrote of the significance of the tertiary bond between man, earth, and heaven in a bit of foreshadowing of the things that would soon follow:

> The words of Amos, who was among the herdmen of Tekoa, which he saw concerning Israel in the days of Uzziah king of Judah, and in the days of Jeroboam the son of Joash king of Israel, two years before the earthquake. And he said, The Lord will roar from Zion, and utter his voice from Jerusalem; and the habitations of the shepherds shall mourn, and the top of Carmel shall wither. (Amos 1:1–2)

Whether Amos was alluding to Uzziah's unrighteous behavior in entering the temple without authorization as the impetus for the eight-plus magnitude earthquake that impacted ancient Israel in 750 BC[7] (often referred to as the "Amos Earthquake") is left to the ages. If the oracles of legend and the prophets of old (as well as a few of the newer ones from our own day) are to be believed, one common thread that appears as a constant reminder is that the events of nature often coincide with the actions of a grieving God, a wicked culture, and a restless world.

One thing is certain: the fact that Amos delivered his speech a full two years before the earthquake leveled most of Judah left the Hebrew culture in shock. As all of Judah was sweeping up the rubble, the idea of altars cracking (Amos 3:14), houses being destroyed (Amos 6:10–11), and the earth itself trembling (Amos 8:8) didn't seem so far removed two years after the shepherd-farmer made his declaration.

Fast-forward two centuries and the apocalyptic tone of Joel suggests the downfall—not just of the land on which the Hebrew kingdom stood—but the very kingdom of Jerusalem itself. Joel prophesied,

> Blow ye the trumpet in Zion, and sound an alarm in my holy mountain: let all the inhabitants of the land tremble: for the day of the Lord cometh, for it is nigh at hand; A day of darkness and of gloominess, a day of clouds and of thick darkness, as the morning spread upon the mountains: a great people and a strong; there hath not been ever the like, neither shall be any more after it, even to the years of many generations. (Joel 2:1–2)

In theory, if you were a Hebrew during Joel's time, life was a lot less complicated. As a people, you'd head into town once a year, go to the temple and give thanks for your crops and livestock, live the law of Moses, raise your family, and stay close to the word of God as it was prescribed by the tribal leaders and according to the Talmud.

In theory.

By consequence, however, Joel, like the prophets before him and those who would follow, saw the destruction of his people—not because of the conquest by another nation (although that didn't help matters), but because of their consistent desire to step out of line with the powers-that-be (a.k.a., "God"), resulting in destruction, captivity, and generations of despair. The shift in control for both the upper and lower kingdoms remained in a constant state of turmoil, and Christian scholars have suggested this similarity can be seen today as people choose to abandon godly principles for worldly trappings (another sign of the last dispensation). John had this to say concerning "the world":

> And now come I to thee; and these things I speak in the world, that they might have my joy fulfilled in themselves. I have given them thy word; and the world hath hated them, because they are not of the world, even as I am not of the world. I pray not that thou shouldest take them out of the world, but that thou shouldest keep them from the evil. They are not of the world, even as I am not of the world. Sanctify them through thy truth: thy word is truth. As thou hast sent me into the world, even so have I also sent them into the world. And for their sakes I sanctify myself, that they also might be sanctified through the truth. (John 17:13–19)

Many religious scholars question the so-called "Israelization" of certain Christian groups because of their close association and desire to be aligned with Israel, which many theologians have considered the original Church of God.

Whether out of necessity or by prophecy, the gathering of Israel has already begun. On May 14, 1948, the nation of Israel was restored to a portion of its original land and has continued to make efforts to extend its locus of influence in the region and throughout the world. Then there's the one-two punch offered by Joel and Luke respectively:

> And I will shew wonders in the heavens and in the earth, blood, and fire, and pillars of smoke. The sun shall be turned into darkness, and the moon into blood, before the great and terrible day of the Lord come. (Joel 2:30–31)

> And I will shew wonders in heaven above, and signs in the earth beneath; blood, and fire, and vapour of smoke. (Acts 2:19)

Some scholars would suggest Joel's prophecy began to be fulfilled on the Day of Pentecost, when the Holy Ghost was left in the world upon the Lord's final Ascension to heaven. Others would suggest that "blood and fire" is a reference to the vengeance that the Lord, upon his final return, will impose on those who betrayed him, in alignment with the activities in ancient Egypt surrounding Passover.

Some factions within Christianity teach that after the return of Jesus, the world will be transformed into a glorified state. This state of existence, they suggest, is the same condition the world was in when God walked with Adam and Eve in the Garden of Eden. Before the final events leading to the sunset of mortality as we know it, several pre-apocryphal events need to take place, as explained by biblical prophets. An important one is the reunion of the nation of Israel, which includes all of the tribes as described in the books of Isaiah and Jeremiah:

> For a small moment have I forsaken thee [Israel]; but with great mercies will I gather thee. (Isaiah 54:7)

> The children of Israel shall come, they and the children of Judah together. . . . They shall ask the way to Zion with their faces thitherward, saying, Come, and let us join ourselves to the Lord. (Jeremiah 50:4–5)

Jeremiah also implies blending Jewish doctrine with the fulfillment of the law of Moses through the life and Atonement of Jesus as he taught during his earthly ministry. Although it might seem as though we're living in a world similar to what has been prophesied, according to the prophecies, this is a picnic compared to what's coming.

With volcanoes darkening a third of modern Europe (and forcing aircraft to be rerouted for days at a time), recurring catastrophic-force hurricanes in the Atlantic, massive earthquakes in Mexico, and wars in the streets and fields, one wonders if Isaiah's words regarding God forsaking his children were extended to all of us who are watching these prophecies unfold today.

———

NOTES

1. *Christianity Today*, "John Nelson Darby: Father of Dispensationalism," http://www .christianitytoday.com/history/people/pastorsandpreachers/john-nelson-darby.html. Accessed April 25, 2018.

2. Bible.org, "Where did the term 'rapture' come from?" https://bible.org/question/where-did-term-8216rapture%E2%80%99-come. Accessed April 25, 2018.

3. *Gospel Principles*, "The Millennium," chapter 45 (Salt Lake City: The Church of Jesus Christ of Latter-day Saints, 1978), 263–67. See https://www.lds.org/languages/eng /content/manual/gospel-principles/chapter-45-the-millennium. Accessed April 25, 2018.

4. Ligonier Ministries, Dr. R. C. Sproul, "The Last Days According to Jesus," https://www .ligonier.org/learn/series/last_days_according_to_jesus/the-millennium-938/. Accessed April 25, 2018.

5. Bible Gateway, Revelation 20, https://www.biblegateway.com/passage/?search= Revelation+20&version=NKJV. Accessed April 25, 2018.

6. Bible Study Tools, "Epiphaneia," https://www.biblestudytools.com/lexicons/greek/nas /epiphaneia.html. Accessed April 25, 2018.

7. Institute for Creation Research, Steven A. Austin, PhD, "The Scientific and Scriptural Impact of Amos' Earthquake," http://www.icr.org/article/scientific-scriptural-impact -amos-earthquake/. Accessed April 25, 2018.

Chapter 30

That Final Great War

—⟨∾⊚∾⟩—

—Revelation 16:16

"War is hell."[1]

When he was speaking at the graduation ceremony of the Michigan Military Academy Class of 1879, noted Union Army General William Tecumseh Sherman referred to the ravages of armed conflict and coined a phrase for the ages, one that has become the standard in describing conflict in the most profound and simplest of terms.

What of the hell described as the final war that would encompass all of man's struggles and conflicts and stand as the ultimate battle, that decisive catastrophic event referred to by Christians as Armageddon?[2]

Perhaps one of the more speculated events in foretelling the Lord's return has been the matter of "wars and rumors of wars" and the fabled Battle of Armageddon as described by the late American Reverend Billy Graham as "a war to eclipse anything the world has ever seen."[3]

The beloved Reverend Graham recounted the book of Revelation like many Christian scholars in anticipation of a continuation of man's penchant for self-destruction, but what if the stage has already been set for Armageddon?

What if it has already begun?

The word *armageddon* originates from the compound Hebrew phrase Har Megiddo[4] in reference to a battle site in ancient Mesopotamia[5] where in a period between 1479 and 1457 BC the Egyptian Pharaoh Thutmose III took on the vassal states of Canaan led by King Kadesh. While many battles have been fought on the plains of Megiddo, this "great war" of its time lasted seven months and was the first of many conflicts fought on the plains of Megiddo (although the term or place of Armageddon never appears in the Old Testament).

History (and religious doctrine of many Christian sects) is replete with references to great wars. The American Civil War, as an example, was often referred to as the "Great War between the North and South," with more than 620,000 soldiers being killed in that war alone. World War I has historically been referred to as the "Great War" and saw an eight-year global conflict involving thirty-two countries and the loss of nearly forty million lives. Anyone who lived through WWII would testify of the profound impact it had on the human race with its global death toll exceeding eighty million.

What, then, of this Armageddon referenced by John in Revelation 16:16?

And he gathered them together into a place called in the Hebrew tongue Armageddon. (Revelation 16:16)

How does John's reference to this great battle correlate with the Lord's return as many Christian leaders[6] from the past two millennia have foretold?

According to accounts in the books of Joel and Isaiah in the Old Testament and Revelation in the New Testament, the last great war of mankind is to take place between two massive armies. The battle includes the armies of Gog and Magog from countries north of Israel.

This final battle, according to Christian tradition, marks the beginning of the end of world conflict. Events preceding the battle of Armageddon are forecast to resemble much of what we are currently seeing running rampant throughout the Middle East. Prophecies of nations collapsing and evil sinking to new levels of malevolence seem to be part of the formula for man's appetite for destruction and serve as the impetus for the End of Days.

Modern-day philosophies and interpretation of revelation suggest that upon the arrival of the risen Messiah, the world will be returned to a state of glorified existence similar to that of the Garden of Eden. This transformation will be necessary to provide safe harbor for those eternal beings (the righteous souls who walked the earth throughout time) who will eventually visit and ultimately inhabit the earth.

But "all hell" has to break loose first.

Many of the Old Testament prophets, including Isaiah, Jeremiah, Ezekiel, Daniel, and Zechariah, referenced some form of final ultimate conflict between global forces in an all-in battle for the liberty of the human race. In Isaiah we read,

Howl ye; for the day of the Lord is at hand; it shall come as a destruction from the Almighty. Therefore shall all hands be faint, and every man's heart shall melt: And they shall be afraid: pangs and sorrows shall take hold of them; they shall be in pain as a woman that travaileth: they shall be amazed one at another; their faces shall be as flames. Behold, the day of the Lord cometh, cruel both with wrath and fierce anger, to lay the land desolate: and he shall destroy the sinners thereof out of it. For the stars of heaven and the constellations thereof shall not give their light: the sun shall be darkened in his going forth, and the moon shall not cause her light to shine. And I will punish the world for their evil, and the wicked for their iniquity; and I will cause the arrogancy of the proud to cease, and will lay low the haughtiness of the terrible. (Isaiah 13:6–11)

Some biblical scholars suggest that Isaiah's reference to "the day of the Lord" being at hand refers to parallel historical events. One refers to a battle in which Babylon (Hebrew captors during Isaiah's time) will fall desolate (which present-day Iraq has already done), and another refers to a modern-day "Babylon" (that has yet to fall).

Babylon in ancient times was the greatest power in the land and soon became a symbol representing powerful nations that ruled with impunity, such as John referred to in his Revelation:

I saw another angel come down from heaven, having great power; and the earth was lightened with his glory. And he cried mightily with a strong voice, saying, Babylon the great is fallen, is fallen, and is become the habitation of devils, and the hold of every foul spirit, and a cage of every unclean and hateful bird. For all nations have drunk of the wine of the wrath of her fornication, and the kings of the earth have committed fornication with her, and the merchants of the earth are waxed rich through the abundance of her delicacies. (Revelation 18:1–3)

While historians suggest that much of Revelation pertains to John's lightly veiled and often encoded[7] grievances toward the empire of Rome (and the ultimate redemption to be provided by the Savior upon his return), scholars suggest that he is also implying the destruction of a great and powerful (and wicked) nation that has come to find itself at odds with God.

With more than four thousand years of conflict surrounding a small area about sixty miles outside of Jerusalem, where generations of Jews, Gentiles, Muslims, and Mesopotamians have laid each other to waste, a common theme would suggest that everybody has it in for Israel, whether symbolic or literally. Thus, the battle with Gog and Magog, as described by the Old Testament Prophet Ezekiel and later by John, will begin (and end) with one final siege of Jerusalem. Unlike the time of the Crusades when Christian kings sought to liberate the Holy Land from its heathen hosts, according to the prophets of old (and a few new ones), the battle for Israel will be for the final redemption of the human race.

The gears, according to some of the signs foretold by Ezekiel and Zechariah, have already been set in motion. Consider the following:

- Israel will be gathered (Ezekiel 36). The modern nation of Israel was made official in 1948.

- Jerusalem will stand as the capital of the Jewish people worldwide (Zechariah 1 & 2). Jerusalem is the recognized capital of the Jewish State, and, at present, even the United States is relocating its embassy from Tel Aviv to Jerusalem in recognition of this fact.

- Israel will become "mighty men, which will tread down their enemies" (Zechariah 10:5). The nation-state of Israel is a nuclear power and is respected as a central force of liberty and independence throughout the Middle East and the world. (Note that amidst current chaos between Syria, Iraq, Palestine, and its surrounding adversaries, Israel remains a tenuous territory of controversy and border conflict.)

Who are these characters Gog and Magog?

Although the name Gog of Ezekiel's time suggests no particular individual, Ezekiel (and later John in his Revelation), suggest that Gog and his land, represented by Magog, symbolize the great Babylonian heretics who would stand against Israel, God, and all that is part of God's plan. And while Jewish eschatology[8] looks to the battle of Gog and Magog as the point where their promised Messiah will finally arrive on the scene and redeem them from their oppressors, Christians look at the battle of Armageddon as man's final conflict before God calls an end to all of the mayhem.

Daniel's prophecy of the coming of a "king of the north"[9] (No, not that one!) with a "great army" to conquer the land has been interpreted to be anyone from Alexander the Great to a yet-to-be identified force.

The prophecies of the Old and New Testaments, as well as current signs of the times, suggest that despite whatever forces may be present to bring upon Israel what are foretold to be its darkest days yet, there's going to be hell to pay for Gog, Magog, and everyone else who stands between Christ and his people.

NOTES

1. Richard Geib's Personal Website, "General William Tecumseh Sherman to the Mayor and Councilmen of Atlanta," http://www.rjgeib.com/thoughts/sherman/sherman-to-burn-atlanta.html. Accessed April 25, 2018.
2. Dictionary.com, "Armageddon," http://www.dictionary.com/browse/armageddon. Accessed April 25, 2018.
3. Billy Graham Evangelistic Association, BGEA Staff, "What is the battle of Armageddon?" https://billygraham.org/answer/what-is-the-battle-of-armageddon/, June 1, 2004. Accessed April 25, 2018.
4. United Church of God, Beyond Today, Darris McNeely, "A Place Called Megiddo: The World's Battleground," https://www.ucg.org/world-news-and-prophecy/a-place-called-megiddo-the-worlds-battleground, February 7, 2006. Accessed April 25, 2018.
5. Eshafim.org, "Thutmose III: The Battle of Megiddo," http://www.reshafim.org.il/ad/egypt/megiddobattle.htm. Accessed April 25, 2018.

6. Bible.org, "Armageddon and the Second Coming of Christ," https://bible.org/seriespage/13-armageddon-and-second-coming-christ. Accessed April 25, 2018.
7. StackExchange, Biblical Hermeneutics, "Was the Revelation written in code to hide it from the Romans?" https://hermeneutics.stackexchange.com/questions/9052/was-the-revelation-written-in-code-to-hide-it-from-the-romans. Accessed April 25, 2018.
8. Jewish Encyclopedia, Kaufmann Kohler, "Eschatology: 'The End of Days,'" http://www.jewishencyclopedia.com/articles/5849-eschatology. Accessed April 25, 2018.
9. See Daniel chapter 11.

CHAPTER 31

THE TIMES OF THE
GENTILES FULFILLED

He shall turn the heart of the fathers to the children,
and the heart of the children to their fathers.

—Malachi 4:6

"The end of the prophets."

That's the last passage written in the Old Testament of the King James Version of the Bible. Whether as a result of the declaration of Malachi's prophecy regarding the earth being consumed by fire in the last days, or because of a passing remark by the biblical councils who assembled the version that has stood as the most widely distributed book of all time, Christian eschatology supposes that in the final days of man those who will not remember the law of Moses[1] or turn the children's hearts to their fathers will be smitten with a curse.

And what was that curse declared by Malachi?

Fire!

> For, behold, the day cometh, that shall burn as an oven; and all the proud, yea, and all that do wickedly, shall be stubble: and the day that cometh shall burn them up, saith the Lord of hosts, that it shall leave them neither root nor branch. But unto you that fear my name shall the Sun of righteousness arise with healing in his wings; and ye shall go forth, and grow up as calves of the stall. And ye shall tread down the wicked; for they shall be ashes under the soles of your feet in the day that I shall do this, saith the Lord of hosts. Remember ye the law of Moses my servant, which I commanded unto him in Horeb for all Israel, with the statutes and judgments. Behold, I will send you Elijah the prophet before the coming of the great and dreadful day of the Lord: And he shall turn the heart of the fathers to the children, and the heart of the children to their fathers, lest I come and smite the earth with a curse. (Malachi 4:1–6)

Malachi's prophecies foretell of the coming destruction of the world. More than two thousand years ago, the Jews thought Malachi's prophecies were coming to pass when a man with the "spirit of Elijah" came forth out of the wilderness. Scholars and many theologians suggest this prophecy was partially fulfilled[2] with John the Baptist. When Jesus himself was asked about this prophecy, he referred to his cousin, John, as fulfillment of that prophecy.

What of the "fire and brimstone" that was foreshadowed?

The old war philosophy of "scorched earth policy" (meaning the burning of an enemy's town and its resources) is also part of the events marking the final stage of the advent of the Second Coming. Based on passages throughout the Old and New Testaments, Christians in almost all sects believe that upon his return, Jesus will use fire to consume the wicked,[3] the prideful, and anyone who chooses not to follow his counsel and his Father's commandments.

Isaiah described the final conflicts in the last days as an epoch of one calamity after another. He prophesied that man himself would become more precious than gold. He wrote,

> For the indignation of the Lord is upon all nations, and his fury upon all their armies: he hath utterly destroyed them, he hath delivered them to the slaughter. Their slain also shall be cast out, and their stink shall come up out of their carcasses, and the mountains shall be melted with their blood. And all the host of heaven shall be dissolved, and the heavens shall be rolled together as a scroll: and all their host shall fall down, as the leaf falleth off from the vine, and as a falling fig from the fig tree. (Isaiah 34:2–4)

This "baptism by fire," referring to the fire by which the earth will be cleansed this second time around (the first was by flood), follows the pattern of people being first baptized by water (as in the case of the flood at the time of Noah) and then by the "fire" of the Holy Spirit. To God, the world itself and all who live on it are alive. As such, it too required cleansing after the fall of man. This cleansing, as in the case of the earth being completely immersed in water, must now be followed with a cleansing by fire if Malachi and the other prophets of old are to be taken literally.

> Therefore hath the curse devoured the earth, and they that dwell therein are desolate: therefore the inhabitants of the earth are burned, and few men left. . . . The mountains quake at him, and the hills melt, and the earth is burned at his presence, yea, the world, and all that dwell therein. . . . But the day of the Lord will come as a thief in the night; in the which the heavens shall pass away with a great noise, and the elements shall melt with fervent heat, the earth also and the works that are therein shall be burned up. (Isaiah 24:6 and 2 Peter 3:10; from the Joseph Smith Translation of the Bible)

Although the term "baptism by fire" is symbolic in the way man receives the gift of the Holy Ghost, it has literal meaning where the world is concerned.

The foreshadowing of the final acts of mankind, also referred to as the "fulfill-ment of the times of the Gentiles,"⁴ is described in prophecy as a global conflict that will culminate with the final return of Jesus Christ. The war that brings to a close the times of the Gentiles, which already has embraced twenty-five hundred years of conflict-centered history, will also mark the last-ditch effort of the adversary to countermand his Father's plan.

Isaiah and Luke saw this final grudge match between the fallen Lucifer and his brother. As recorded in the writings of these men,

> How art thou fallen from heaven, O Lucifer, son of the morning! How art thou cut down to the ground, which didst weaken the nations! . . . And he said unto them, I beheld Satan as lightning fall from heaven. (Isaiah 14:2; Luke 10:18)

Although the past two-thousand-plus years might seem like the bad guys are win-ning, John's revelation of Jesus binding his fallen brother puts no finer point on the triumph of righteousness over evil. John prophesied,

> I saw an angel coming down from heaven, having the key to the bottomless pit and a great chain in his hand. He laid hold of the dragon, that serpent of old, who is the Devil and Satan, and bound him for a thousand years; and he cast him into the bottomless pit, and shut him up, and set a seal on him, so that he should deceive the nations no more, till the thousand years should be fulfilled. (Revelation 20:1–3)

Some religious scholars suggest a repeat of Jesus's mortal ministry, since someone with the spirit of Elijah will once again herald the coming (or return) of the Savior in glory. We see this in the ancient prophet Zechariah's words. He writes that the heart of Ephraim "shall rejoice in the Lord" and "Jerusalem [will become] a burdensome stone for all people: all that burden themselves with it shall be cut in pieces, though all the people of the earth be gathered together against it." (See Zechariah 10:7; 12:3.)

Whatever the conditions of the time—and we know things are going to get a lot worse before they get really worse—we can conclude from Isaiah's prophecies about the earth passing, the sun and moon darkening, and a new earth coming to pass ("and the former shall not be remembered" [Isaiah 62]) that the days of Armageddon are not too far off. We can be prepared for these events if we know what to look for, how to plan, and, as the psalmists have attested, how to live. If we are prepared, we need not fear. In the words of the psalmist:

> Teach us to number our days, that we may apply our hearts unto wisdom. Return, O Lord, how long? And let it repent thee concerning thy servants. O satisfy us early with thy mercy; that we may rejoice and be glad all our days. . . . He shall cover thee with his feathers, and under his wings shalt thou trust: his truth shall be thy shield and buckler. Thou shalt not be afraid for the terror by night; nor for the arrow that flieth

by day; nor for the pestilence that walketh in darkness; nor for the destruction that wasteth at noonday. A thousand shall fall at thy side, and ten thousand at thy right hand; but it shall not come nigh thee. Only with thine eyes shalt thou behold and see the reward of the wicked. Because thou hast made the Lord, which is my refuge, even the most High, thy habitation; there shall no evil befall thee, neither shall any plague come nigh thy dwelling. For he shall give his angels charge over thee, to keep thee in all thy ways. (Psalms 90:12–14; 91:4–11)

Would it be a surprise to anyone who studies the scriptures and the foretelling of man's ultimate demise that so many prophets (ancient and modern) spent a great deal of time focusing on the End of Days and the final battle before the return of the Prince of Peace? As a tenet of both Christianity and Judaism, Isaiah interpreted (as well as other prophets who followed) God's final solution as a time when the "kings of the earth, and the great men, and the rich men, and the chief captains, and the mighty men, and every bondman, and every free man [will hide] themselves in the dens and in the rocks of the mountains" (Revelation 6:15).

With stars falling from the heavens and the moon turning the color of blood, things don't appear to be getting any better for the human race as the last days unfold. Jerusalem will be on the brink of collapse, the global death toll will be at an all-time high, and an assortment of plagues, pestilences, and greater calamities are planned for the last days according to the apocalyptic prophecies of so many former (and current) religious sages.

Upon the Savior's return, Christianity teaches that there will be a reckoning of souls, meaning that the righteous will be united with Jesus at his coming, being spared God's angry wrath upon the world. But for those who have chosen wickedness as a way of life, prophets throughout time have warned that things will get pretty hot.

NOTES

1. IAUA End Time Ministry, Third Elijah Message, "The Law of Moses," http://www .thirdelijahmessage.info/MosesLaw.html, 2015. Accessed April 25, 2018.
2. Doctrine.org, Don Samdahl, "John the Baptist as Elijah," https://doctrine.org/john -the-baptist-as-elijah, December 13, 2012. Accessed April 25, 2018.
3. OpenBible, "God Will Destroy Earth by Fire," https://www.openbible.info/topics /god_will_destroy_earth_by_fire, 2018. Accessed April 25, 2018.
4. Bible.org, "The Times of the Gentiles," https://bible.org/article/times-gentiles, 2018. Accessed April 25, 2018.

CHAPTER 32

AND HE SHALL REIGN
FOREVER AND EVER

They shall see the Son of man coming in the clouds of heaven with power and great glory.

—Matthew 24:30

To Christians around the world, the penultimate purpose and objective of the life of Jesus Christ was found in his death upon the cross, as recorded in the New Testament Gospels. It's not every day that a man is born into the world, endures years of poverty (by his own choice), and then suffers torture and death—also by his own choice. But Jesus was such a man. His greater purpose was to freely die, while also having the power to raise up his own life and restore it, all for the sake of humanity.

Modern-day revelation, and some Christian sects, would argue that the most significant aspect of Jesus's life wasn't his death on the cross but rather in those few hours he spent praying in the Garden of Gethsemane[1] the night before he was taken to Golgotha.

With this shift in focus, away from the actual death of Jesus to the sanctified service he provided for all mankind (that being to pray for, suffer for, and endure the pain of the fallen human race), the Atonement itself becomes the single most important event in the life of Christ. During his time in Gethsemane, Jesus—the literal Son of God—pleaded with his Father to consider removing the burden he was to endure there. In the end, however, Jesus accepted the will of the one who sent him, and, as a result, the pressure and strain of bearing the literal burden of all mankind was so intense that Jesus sweat drops of blood.[2]

At the end of his brief visit back on earth after his Resurrection, scripture documents that Jesus assembled his Apostles one final time.[3] He told them that he would leave them for a while, and, like so many parables of vineyards, that he would return at a designated time after the world had the chance to ripen a bit longer. Now, almost two thousand years since Jesus's departure, when many would suggest that the "fruit" has fermented to a point of decay, the Christian world looks anxiously to the day when Jesus will return.

Christian theology supports the notion that the Second Coming of Christ will mark the closure of the final chapter of the mortal probation of mankind, and Jesus's return has been the subject of extensive discussion almost since he left. His return has been called the "Great and Dreadful Day,"[4] "Rapture,"[5] and "End of Days."[6]

Although many cultures today and throughout history have claimed to know when the Lord will return, the scriptures record in the Gospel of Mark that even Christ himself does not know the day God will send him back to us.

> Heaven and earth shall pass away: but my words shall not pass away. But of that day and that hour knoweth no man, no, not the angels which are in heaven, neither the Son, but the Father. Take ye heed, watch and pray: for ye know not when the time is. (Mark 13:31–33)

As discussed in a previous chapter, everyone seems to have an insider track on the ultimate Christian events corresponding with the Second Coming of Christ. Philosophers, popes, prophets, and even a few politicians along the way have pondered on the return of Christ. Books have been written about it, songs sung, and plenty of wailing and gnashing of teeth has occurred over false alarms throughout history. While many religious factions throughout history have their own take on the final disposition of mankind, of all three of the Abrahamic religions (Judaism, Christianity, and Islam), Christians have our own unique, almost obsessive, fascination with global mortality.

The advent of the Lord's return often begs one ultimate question—perhaps more of a curiosity—and that has to do with whether anybody can extrapolate an ETA for Jesus. While philosophers and scholars might want to debate the time line of Christ returning from the heavens, even the Lord told us he would be the last to know when it was time to go.

However, the occurrence of the following eight key events is alluded to as being essential prior to his return:

1. The gospel will be preached to all nations
2. Great tribulation, wars, and rumors of wars
3. Drought and famine
4. Disease and pestilence
5. Opposing religions will prevail
6. Jerusalem will hang in the balance
7. Signs in the heavens

1. The gospel will be preached to all nations—While Jesus sat on the Mount of Olives, his Apostles engaged him on the matter of his ultimate return to them and what they should know regarding the world and his message. His answer:

And many false prophets shall rise, and shall deceive many. And because iniquity shall abound, the love of many shall wax cold. . . . And this gospel of the kingdom shall be preached in all the world for a witness unto all nations; and then shall the end come. (Matthew 24:11–12, 14)

2. Great tribulation, wars, and rumors of wars—The Gospel of Matthew includes Jesus's discussion with his disciples about the state of the world prior to his return, referring to it as "the abomination of desolation." The world has bathed itself in bloodshed since Cain rose up and slew his brother. The magnitude by which we kill each other, however, has risen exponentially, as was examined in chapter 30, when we tallied the modern death toll of two world wars in excess of one hundred million, not to mention the widespread coverage of the increase in mass shootings—even children killing children! Jesus himself shared this foreshadowing:

Many shall come in my name, saying, I am Christ; and shall deceive many. And ye shall hear of wars and rumours of wars: see that ye be not troubled: for all these things must come to pass, but the end is not yet. For nation shall rise against nation, and kingdom against kingdom: and there shall be famines, and pestilences, and earthquakes, in divers places. All these are the beginning of sorrows. . . . Then shall be great tribulation, such as was not since the beginning of the world to this time, no, nor ever shall be. (Matthew 24:5–8, 21)

3. Drought and famine—Two calamities that have historical context in biblical times as well as modern day are the lack of moisture in the land, which usually results in a scarcity of food. Lack of water in the soil means plants dry up and crops die. Of all natural disasters, a "withering drought"[7] is only second in economic impact to a hurricane.[8] While the Bible is replete with stories of tribes waging war against each other, as well as on the elements, modern history has experienced droughts so devastating (such as the Great Dust Bowl of the 1930s, the Northern Great Plains in the late 1980s, and Syria since 2007) that the land was permanently scarred, forcing entire communities to vanish. When crops and livestock die, people don't lag too far behind. It was as true in the days of Moses as it is now, and Jesus warned that prior to his return there would be famines. John also points to a future scarcity in supplies:

And when he had opened the third seal, I heard the third beast say, Come and see. And I beheld, and lo a black horse; and he that sat on him had a pair of balances in his hand. And I heard a voice in the midst of the four beasts say, A measure of wheat for a penny, and three measures of barley for a penny; and see thou hurt not the oil and the wine. (Revelation 6:5–6)

4. Disease and pestilence—In war-ravaged places, there is often little left of conditions that sustain any quality of life. Compounding such problems, in the absence of water and in the presence of mass starvation, other catastrophes often shadow the dead

and dying. Jesus mentioned (and John reiterated) the increase in natural calamities in the world, like back-to-back-to-back Category-Five hurricanes in the Gulf, massive landslides, perpetual winter "nor'easters," volcanoes, and wildfires burning out of control. Flooding, fires, and droughts have always figured into God's rebuke of his children. Even the Old Testament books of Joel and Zechariah refer to earthquakes that have since been scientifically tracked to large-scale natural disasters from those respective periods. Moreover, both Matthew and Mark record that the Lord not only pointed to the sky from where he would someday return in glory, but he also looked to the earth itself for a sign of his impending arrival. Consider the following verses found in Matthew's and Mark's records:

> There shall be famines, and pestilences, and earthquakes, in divers places. . . . For nation shall rise against nation, and kingdom against kingdom: and there shall be earthquakes in divers places, and there shall be famines and troubles: these are the beginnings of sorrows. (Matthew 24:7; Mark 13:8)

5. Opposing religions will prevail—While Christianity remains the largest religious faction in the world, and the largest of the three Abrahamic sects, it represents less than one-third of the global population,[9] with all other non-Christian faiths comprising the balance of the current population. In his three opening sermons found in the book of Deuteronomy, Moses admonishes the people of Israel to remain close to the word of God and not become deceived by people (leaders) who would rise up among them and preach false principles that would appear to be truth. Centuries later, Peter counsels of similar false teachings. He writes,

> If there arise among you a prophet, or a dreamer of dreams, and giveth thee a sign or a wonder, and the sign or the wonder come to pass, whereof he spake unto thee, saying, Let us go after other gods, which thou hast not known, and let us serve them; Thou shalt not hearken unto the words of that prophet, or that dreamer of dreams: for the Lord your God proveth you, to know whether ye love the Lord your God with all your heart and with all your soul. Ye shall walk after the Lord your God, and fear him, and keep his commandments, and obey his voice, and ye shall serve him, and cleave unto him. . . . But there were false prophets also among the people, even as there shall be false teachers among you, who privily shall bring in damnable heresies, even denying the Lord that bought them, and bring upon themselves swift destruction. And many shall follow their pernicious ways; by reason of whom the way of truth shall be evil spoken of. (Deuteronomy 13:1–4; 2 Peter 2:1–2)

6. Jerusalem will hang in the balance—Almost since the beginning of its inception as a nation-state in 1948, Israel has been the center of Middle East controversy. While these social, cultural, and political burdens have been the bitter companion of Israel since Moses brought them out of Egypt, Jerusalem remains the epicenter of conflict and controversy since it is considered a holy city by all three Abrahamic religions. But whether the Dome of

the Rock or the Mount of Olives, the prophecies of old—from Moses and Zechariah down to Luke and Jesus himself—about Jerusalem being "surrounded by armies on all sides" may be closer to reality than just an idea. Zechariah, and later Luke, prophesied,

> Behold, the day of the Lord cometh, and thy spoil shall be divided in the midst of thee. For I will gather all nations against Jerusalem to battle; and the city shall be taken, and the houses rifled, and the women ravished; and half of the city shall go forth into captivity, and the residue of the people shall not be cut off from the city. Then shall the Lord go forth, and fight against those nations, as when he fought in the day of battle. And his feet shall stand in that day upon the mount of Olives, which is before Jerusalem on the east, and the mount of Olives shall cleave in the midst thereof toward the east and toward the west, and there shall be a very great valley; and half of the mountain shall remove toward the north, and half of it toward the south. . . . And when ye shall see Jerusalem compassed with armies, then know that the desolation thereof is nigh. Then let them which are in Judaea flee to the mountains; and let them which are in the midst of it depart out; and let not them that are in the countries enter thereinto. For these be the days of vengeance, that all things which are written may be fulfilled . . . and Jerusalem shall be trodden down of the Gentiles, until the times of the Gentiles be fulfilled. (Zechariah 14:1–4; Luke 21:20–22, 24)

7. Signs in the heavens—Through the closing decades of the twentieth century and into the current season, there have been numerous astronomical phenomena, including the return of Halley's Comet in 1986 and the additional comets Hale-Bopp in 1995 and Hyakutake the following year. In the summer of 2017, North America and the United States saw the longest-lasting total solar eclipse on record, with subsequent eclipses due to appear in 2024, 2045, 2052, 2078, and 2099. The Aurora Borealis (Northern Lights) has increased in activity,[10] appearing as far south as the Caribbean. Although such phenomena have been attributed to increased solar activity and good old-fashioned coincidence, Jesus and his prophets offer a different perspective. Matthew and John recorded the following:

> Immediately after the tribulation of those days shall the sun be darkened, and the moon shall not give her light, and the stars shall fall from heaven, and the powers of the heavens shall be shaken: And then shall appear the sign of the Son of man in heaven: and then shall all the tribes of the earth mourn, and they shall see the Son of man coming in the clouds of heaven with power and great glory. And he shall send his angels with a great sound of a trumpet, and they shall gather together his elect from the four winds, from one end of heaven to the other. . . . And the sun became black as sackcloth of hair, and the moon became as blood; And the stars of heaven fell unto the earth. (Matthew 24:29–31; Revelation 6:12–13)

In previous chapters, we looked at the events leading up to and including the time known as the Apocalypse and the subsequent millennium of calm that follows the so-called "Great and Dreadful Day." Although even Jesus doesn't know the day of his return, for those who study his words and recognize the signs of the times, his impending arrival should not come as a surprise.

————

NOTES

1. Facing the Façade, Caleb Henry, "Gethsemane vs. Golgotha: Is the Cross Really That Important?" http://anewregress.blogspot.com/2011/05/gethsemane-vsgolgotha-is-cross -really.html, May 23, 2011. Accessed April 26, 2018.

2. *Christian Courier*, Wayne Jackson, "The Agony of Gethsemane," https://www.christian courier.com/articles/421-agony-of-gethsemane-the. Accessed April 26, 2018.

3. Answers in Genesis, Dr. Elizabeth Mitchell, "The Sequence of Christ's Post Resurrection Appearances," https://answersingenesis.org/jesus-christ/resurrection/the-sequence-of -christs-post-resurrection-appearances/, March 21, 2012. Accessed April 26, 2018.

4. *Old Testament Gospel Doctrine Teacher's Manual*, lesson 48, "The Great and Dreadful Day of the Lord," Zechariah 10–14 and Malachi (Salt Lake City: The Church of Jesus Christ of Latter-day Saints, 1996) 225–29. See https://www.lds.org/languages/eng/content /manual/old-testament-gospel-doctrine-teachers-manual/lesson-48. Accessed April 26, 2018.

5. BeliefNet, Lesli White, "6 Things Every Christian Should Know about the Rapture," http://www.beliefnet.com/faiths/christianity/6-things-every-christian-should-know -about-the-rapture.aspx. Accessed April 26, 2018.

6. *National Geographic*, Matthew Paul Turner, "The Different Meanings of End of Days," http://channel.nationalgeographic.com/the-story-of-god-with-morgan-freeman/articles /the-different-meanings-of-end-of-days/. Accessed April 26, 2018.

7. History Channel, Jesse Greenspan, "7 Withering Droughts," https://www.history.com /news/7-withering-droughts, June 30, 2015. Accessed April 26, 2018.

8. List25, Theodoros II, "25 Most Severe Droughts Ever Recorded," https://list25.com/25 -most-severe-droughts-ever-recorded/, March 18, 2016. Accessed April 26, 2018.

9. Wikipedia, "Major Religious Groups," https://en.wikipedia.org/wiki/Major_religious _groups, 2018. Accessed April 26, 2018.

10. *Forbes*, WhoaScience, Jillian Scudder, "How Far South Could You See the Aurora with a Perfect Solar Storm?" https://www.forbes.com/sites/jillianscudder/2017/01/14 /astroquizzical-aurora-solar-storm/#5e7e4be76bdf, January 14, 2017. Accessed April 26, 2018.

CHAPTER 33

RESTITUTION OF ALL THINGS

The voice of weeping shall be no more heard in her.

—Isaiah 65:19

The end is near!

No study of Christian eschatology could be concluded without examining our philosophy on how mankind is to be dealt with after the Lord's return.

Following the thousand-year period, or the Millennium, in which Jesus presides over the world's religious affairs, there will be one last battle between Satan and the followers of Christ. According to modern-day revelation, in this final decisive and epic confrontation, the good guys win, with Satan and his minions finally being cast out of man's presence forever. (Sounds like the makings of a *great* movie!)

With Satan out of the picture and the righteous followers of God (both living and dead) finding divine refuge, the world will be transformed into a glorified state like it was when God walked with Adam and Eve. Modern-day revelation proposes that all people who have ever lived on the earth will be resurrected and judged, with each individual being granted an eternal reward based on his or her obedience to God during mortality.

Not everyone lives at the same level of obedience. As a consequence, and as his divine restitution is being meted out, not everyone will receive the same rewards upon the return of Christ.

The notion that "one size fits all" doesn't work when it comes to spiritual rewards and punishments, and contrary to a common belief that merely accepting Jesus as one's personal Savior is sufficient for eternal life, there's more to eternal life beyond "salvation." True, the Atonement guarantees a resurrection for everyone, but what happens when we meet our Maker, according to New Testament authors as well as Jesus himself, depends on how we lived in mortality and goes beyond the Atonement of our soul. The prophets and the Savior himself teach that

Yea, a man may say, Thou hast faith, and I have works: shew me thy faith without
thy works, and I will shew thee my faith by my works. . . . In my Father's house are
many mansions: if it were not so, I would have told you. I go to prepare a place for
you. And if I go and prepare a place for you, I will come again, and receive you unto
myself; that where I am, there ye may be also. . . . There are also celestial bodies, and
bodies terrestrial: but the glory of the celestial is one, and the glory of the terrestrial
is another. There is one glory of the sun, and another glory of the moon, and another
glory of the stars: for one star differeth from another star in glory. So also is the resurrection of the dead. (James 2:18; John 14:2–3; 1 Corinthians 15:40–42)

Three days after Christ was crucified, he was resurrected, reuniting a glorified body
with his eternal spirit. Christianity teaches that until that time, no one had ever es-
caped the bonds of death. That event marked the beginning of the First Resurrection. In
1 Thessalonians we read,

For the Lord himself will come down from heaven with a shout of command, with
the voice of the archangel, and with the trumpet of God, and the dead in Christ will
rise first. (1 Thessalonians 4:16)

When Christ was resurrected, many other righteous spirits came forth from the
grave, according to ancient scripture. Matthew wrote,

And the graves were opened; and many bodies of the saints which slept arose, and
came out of the graves after his resurrection, and went into the holy city, and appeared unto many. (Matthew 27:52–53)

Based on the First Resurrection of Christ, we are now living during this period,
which started with Jesus himself and will yet continue after his return, until all of the
righteous souls are brought forth from the grave.

It is in this notion, that of a "restitution in all things," that the scriptures teach that
all people who lived on the earth are entitled to be resurrected. However, the scriptures
also note that not all people receive the same reward, and, as such, they are not all
raised from the dead at the same time. The First Resurrection is the time when the most
righteous of souls are raised up to join Christ during his millennial reign on the earth
and will reign with him in an eternal state of glory.

The psalmists, Isaiah, Jeremiah, Ezekiel, and almost all of the recorded Old and
New Testament prophets wrote extensive passages with reference to the Lord delivering
his people from the torments of the adversary, the demon, the dragon, Perdition, and
other nefarious titles for Lucifer.

The Lord shall send the rod of thy strength out of Zion: rule thou in the midst of
thine enemies. . . . In the last days, . . . the mountain of the Lord's house shall be

established in the top of the mountains, and shall be exalted above the hills; and all nations shall flow unto it. . . . Behold, the days come, saith the Lord, that I will raise unto David a righteous Branch, and a King shall reign and prosper, and shall execute judgment and justice in the earth. . . . In that day, . . . the Lord shall punish the host of the high ones that are on high, and the kings of the earth upon the earth. And they shall be gathered together, as prisoners are gathered in the pit, and shall be shut up in the prison, and after many days shall they be visited. (Psalm 110:2; Isaiah 2:2; Jeremiah 23:5; Isaiah 24:21–22)

As part of this restitution, the Bible tells us of numerous ways in which we can prepare ahead of time and how we can recognize the signs and events that will take place before and after the Lord's return. Among the many indications, here are four more commonly accepted events:

1. Jesus will reign as supreme leader
2. Satan will be bound
3. Death will be different
4. All truth will be brought forth

1. Jesus will reign as supreme leader—During his mortal ministry, Jesus made it clear that upon his return in glory, he will be the one in charge of all things. The following passages from Matthew reaffirm this conviction of the Savior's redemption of the human race (although probably not a good time for the "goats!"):

When the Son of man shall come in his glory, and all the holy angels with him, then shall he sit upon the throne of his glory: And before him shall be gathered all nations: and he shall separate them one from another, as a shepherd divideth his sheep from the goats: And he shall set the sheep on his right hand, but the goats on the left. Then shall the King say unto them on his right hand, Come, ye blessed of my Father, inherit the kingdom prepared for you from the foundation of the world. (Matthew 25:31–34)

After judging the world, Jesus is foretold to oversee a thousand years of global peace:

And I saw thrones, and they sat upon them, and judgment was given unto them . . . and they lived and reigned with Christ a thousand years. (Revelation 20:4)

2. Satan will be bound—Just as God cannot abide in unclean places, Satan cannot stand in the holy presence of God. Chapter 20 in the book of Revelation is the only place in the Bible that mentions the period called the Millennium. In this portion of John's Apocalypse, he refers to an angel descending from heaven, which many biblical scholars infer to mean Jesus himself.

> And I saw an angel come down from heaven, having the key of the bottomless pit and a great chain in his hand. And he laid hold on the dragon, that old serpent, which is the Devil, and Satan, and bound him a thousand years, And cast him into the bottomless pit, and shut him up, and set a seal upon him, that he should deceive the nations no more, till the thousand years should be fulfilled. (Revelation 20:1–3)

One of the most stark realities defined in divine law is that wickedness cannot stand in the presence of God, and in some ironic sense of contrast, wherever the embodied Christ appeared, it was always those wicked souls who first recognized him. Both Mark and Luke relate the following:

> A man with an unclean spirit . . . cried out, Let us alone; what have we to do with thee, thou Jesus of Nazareth? Art thou come to destroy us? I know thee who thou art, the Holy One of God. And Jesus rebuked him, saying, Hold thy peace, and come out of him. . . . And when the devil had thrown him in the midst, he came out of him, and hurt him not. (Mark 1:23–25; Luke 4:35)

In Matthew, Jesus notes that when unclean spirits are cast out, it is a sign that the Kingdom of God has come forth.

The prophets (old and new) foresaw that upon the Savior's triumphant return to reign on earth, Satan's illegitimate control and influence over the world would be removed and transferred to the legitimate Lord, who—as Isaiah prophesied—would bear the "government upon his shoulders."

3. Death will be different—Again, in Revelation chapter 20, John prophesies of a time when, upon the return of Jesus and at the close of the First Resurrection, the dead will not rise "until the thousand years [are] finished." Further, and often misunderstood, is the notion that death will not be present in the time of the millennial man. Not true. Isaiah references a time when children will grow to a ripe old age. He wrote,

> There shall be no more thence an infant of days, nor an old man that hath not filled his days: for the child shall die an hundred years old; . . . And they shall build houses, and inhabit them; and they shall plant vineyards, and eat the fruit of them. (Isaiah 65:20–21)

Christian scholars believe that while death will surely come to pass for all of us, Isaiah's reference to children living out their lives to the full measure of their productivity and potential suggests that death will come only after the men and women living on the earth have had the opportunity to learn, work, live, and love, along with whatever else might be part of a quality life in a world where the resurrected Christ is in charge.

Some Christian scholars also suggest the absence of sadness and misery. Verses 18, 19, and 25 of Isaiah chapter 65 reference a time beyond the Millennium:

Be ye glad and rejoice for ever in that which I create. . . . The voice of weeping shall be no more heard in her, nor the voice of crying. . . . They shall not hurt nor destroy in all my holy mountain, saith the Lord. (Isaiah 65:18–19, 25)

Interpretations of these passages might suggest that Isaiah is not looking just to millennial times. His references to the wolf dwelling with the lamb, the leopard that shall lie down with the kid, and the calf and the young lion and fatling together (see Isaiah 11:6), in addition to an absence of pain and destruction, suggest a time during Christ's eternal reign.

4. All truth will be brought forth—While we live in an age when information can be found on myriad topics and virtually everywhere the Internet can be accessed, there is still much about the gospel plan that God has yet to reveal to the world. Moreover, there are still places in the world where Christianity is fragmented in its belief system. In his writings regarding the restitution of all things, the Apostle John describes how the gospel will be spread across the land:

And I saw another angel fly in the midst of heaven, having the everlasting gospel to preach unto them that dwell on the earth, and to every nation, and kindred, and tongue, and people, saying with a loud voice, Fear God, and give glory to him; for the hour of his judgment is come: and worship him that made heaven, and earth, and the sea, and the fountains of waters. (Revelation 14:6–7)

And finally, While the Christian populations throughout history have long awaited the return of Jesus, his imminent reign of peace and justice has been foretold for thousands of years, even before his mortal ministry.

When Jesus was born into the world, few people were aware of the significance of his birth. Scholars, civic leaders, priests, and prophets have interpreted the foretelling of his return. While no one (not even Jesus) knows the specific details relating to his return, Christianity has a pretty good idea of what to do to prepare for his return so they "also [be] ready, for in such an hour as ye think not, the Son of Man cometh" (Matthew 1:48; Joseph Smith Translation of the Bible).

EPILOGUE

W ow. We're done!

If you made it this far, you'll no doubt know that there's more to the study of the Second Coming than what is mentioned in these pages.

What is certain, however, is that the time will surely come when all people will stand at the judgment bar and make an accounting for how they lived, loved, and shared what they learned.

For someone who has been writing for more than forty years, this was the most challenging project I've ever undertaken. While the subject of the Second Coming has been well argued and perhaps overdocumented, surmising on which biblical passages and historical accounts to include in support of one particular perspective over another often felt like I was trying to herd a flock of birds in a windstorm.

I wanted this publication to be released during the four-year cycle of Bible study in The Church of Jesus Christ of Latter-day Saints and to possibly offer a blend of spiritual and secular interpretation of key topics that pertain to the relevance and pertinence of the timing of what foreshadows the Second Coming of the Savior. Whether such goals were accomplished will remain subjective, but suffice to say, the growing interest in the Lord's return doesn't seem to be receding.

Let's hope we can all accomplish what needs to be done before the clock stops ticking!

ABOUT THE AUTHOR

Drew Williams has been dedicated to studying Jewish and Christian philosophies since he was a boy. Being fascinated with stories from the bible at an early age, because of his grandmother, who used to read Bible stories to him, Drew has spent more than a half century studying biblical and civil histories.

After his grandmother passed away when Drew was nine years old, he became even more interested in reading and learning about ancient civilizations and their relationship with God. Spending his youth attending more than a dozen schools in states throughout the South and Midwest, Drew spent much of his childhood alone, pondering the nature of man and God's involvement in the course of advancing the human condition.

In 1985, after converting to Mormonism while serving in the United States Navy, Drew moved to Utah to attend Brigham Young University, where he graduated with undergraduate degrees in journalism and English.

As a photojournalist for the Navy, and later as a documentary producer and lecturer on infrastructure security, Drew lived and studied in countries throughout Europe, Asia, South America, and the Middle East.

Drew has a master's degree in homeland security from the George Washington University, with an emphasis on political violence and terrorism and is currently working on doctorate programs on defense studies and educational leadership.

Author of one of the multimillion-copy, best-selling Complete Idiots Guides, as well as hundreds of news articles over his forty-year career as a writer, Drew still enjoys discovering what he calls "unlocking the mysteries of the biblical authors" to learn how their writings foreshadow modern times.

Scan to visit

www.aboutdrewwilliams.com